WITH
THE
ADEPTS

*An Adventure
Among the Rosicrucians*

Franz Hartmann, M.D.

Foreword by R. A. Gilbert

Ibis Press
An Imprint of Nicolas-Hays, Inc.
Berwick, Maine

First published in 2003 by Ibis Press
An Imprint of Nicolas-Hays, Inc.
P. O. Box 1126
Berwick, ME 03901-1126
www.nicolashays.com

Distributed to the trade by
Red Wheel/Weiser, LLC
P. O. Box 612
York Beach, ME 03910-0612
www.redwheelweiser.com

Library of Congress Cataloging-in-Publication Data available. ISBN 089254-076-1

Cover design by Alden Cole. Cover art adapted from details of 17th-century engravings from the title pages of *Le Voyage des princes fortunez* and *Le Tableau des riches inventions* by François Beroalde de Verville, engraved by Leonard Gaulthier and Thomas Le Leu.

Printed in the United States of America
BJ

09	08	07	06	05	04	03
7	6	5	4	3	2	1

The paper used in this publication meets the minimum requirements of the American National Standard for Information Sciences—Permanence of Paper for Printed Library Materials Z39.48–1992 (R1997).

CONTENTS

PREFACE

THE following account of a psychic experience has been gathered from notes handed to me by a friend, a writer of considerable repute. Whether the adventures told therein are to be regarded as a dream, or an actual experience on the astral plane, I must leave to the reader to judge.

F. H.

INTRODUCTION

With the Adepts: An Adventure Among the Rosicrucians was Franz Hartmann's third published book and his first work of fiction (except in the eyes of his more hostile critics, who considered almost *all* his works fiction). It also constitutes what might be termed "reflective autobiography." The setting of *With the Adepts* is decidedly Western, both geographically and spiritually, and the text illustrates clearly the beginning of Hartmann's journey back to his spiritual roots in the Western Hermetic Tradition, and away from H.P. Blavatsky's eclectic form of esoteric Buddhism.

As this personal "way of return" gathered pace, so Hartmann's critics within the Theosophical Society attacked his character. Beatrice Hastings denounced his "acid" tongue, and Blavatsky herself stated that, "The magnetism of that man is sickening; his lying beastly; . . . his intrigues unaccountable." Worse still was Rudolf Steiner's claim that Hartmann offered W.Q. Judge the solution to his lament that he never received apported letters from the Masters—writing the letters himself and having Hartmann climb on a chair and drop them on Judge's head! In the theosophical viewpoint, such mocking of the Masters was blasphemy. But was Hartmann truly a self-seeking cynic, or is this a false image painted by hostile critics? The answers to such questions will be found by looking at the course of his life.

Franz Hartmann was born at Donauwerth in the German state of Bavaria, on November 22, 1838, and raised in the nearby city of Kempten. He was educated at the University of Munich with the intention of following his father's career as a medical practitioner. This he did, but secular education also introduced him to the materialist authors of his day and led him to reject the traditional Catholicism in which he had been brought up. Eventually his new-found agnosticism would also pass away, but his return to Western spirituality was to be a long and painful process.

His inquiring mind ought to have fitted Hartmann for an academic career, but he was also blessed—or cursed—with an impulsive and restless nature, and he could never have rested content in the academic world. Thus it was that in 1865, after completing his medical studies, Hartmann took up the post of physician on an emigrant ship from Le Havre to New York. By his own account he loved the sea, but the New World fascinated him, once he had arrived in it. He visited the Niagara Falls and then travelled to St. Louis to "make myself useful," as he put it, during a cholera epidemic. For five years he practiced medicine at St. Louis, where he became an American citizen, but then went south in search of the sun and ended up in Vera Cruz. Mexico delighted him but he could not make a living and he returned to the United States in 1871 to set up in medical practice at New Orleans. There he remained for two years, during which time he discovered Spiritualism and studied "spiritual phenomena" first hand; but his "desire for change and adventures" unsettled him and in 1873 he set off for the "Wild West."

It proved to be wild indeed, and Hartmann noted that "my services for holding inquests were sometimes more in demand than my aid in attending the wounded." For five years he remained in Texas, enjoying life on the prairies—marred only by the death of his wife after seven months of marriage. Hartmann's next stop was Colorado, where he spent a further five years. Here he felt at home because the Rocky Mountains reminded him of his "beloved Bavarian Alps," and perhaps they reminded him, too, of the traditional occupation of the gnomes about whom he would later write, for he also acquired a gold and silver mine near Georgetown. This proved to be wholly worthless and he abandoned mining to return to medicine.

While in Colorado he also revived his involvement with the spirits, working with mediums but never embracing Spiritualism as a creed. His own view was that these phenomena were probably not always caused by the spirits of departed human beings, and that they surely often originated in occult but intelligent forces or powers at present unknown to us.

Much the same approach was to be found in Madame Blavatsky's journal, *The Theosophist*, which Hartmann discovered in 1883. In the first issue that he read was an article "describing the sevenfold constitution of man and the seven principles in nature." This so delighted him that he immediately sought to meet H.P.B. in person. He was invited to Adyar and set off for India via California, delayed only by the charms of a young woman in San Francisco. Fortunately for the occult world, "old Madame Blavatsky and spirituality" were the victors in the struggle against sensuality, and on December 4, 1883, Franz Hartmann arrived in Madras. He was welcomed by H.P.B., became a nominal Buddhist, and on Christmas Day was favored with a letter from the Master Morya. But all was not well in the theosophical paradise.

Letters from the Masters were commonplace at Adyar, but their odd method of delivery, by "precipitation," aroused suspicion and derision on the part of Madame Blavatsky's critics. Hartmann, however, was eager for such communications and delighted when they began to arrive. He received ten letters in all, seven from Morya and three from Koot Hoomi, but to the objective reader none of them can be said to have contained anything of philosophical or spiritual significance. In addition to the letters, Hartmann received a signed photograph of

Morya and was also "so fortunate as to see the Master myself in his astral body."

Thus favored and enthused, Hartmann became a principal defender, in print, of the reality of the Mahatmas and their phenomena. He criticized Arthur Lillie's *Koot Hoomi Unveiled*, and wrote a "Report of Observations" attempting to rebut the damning charges of trickery made against H.P.B. by Mme. Coulomb. This report would have been more effective if had he not also been under suspicion of double-dealing on his own part. A letter, signed "Dr. F. Hartmann" and addressed to Mme. Coulomb had come into Col. Olcott's hands. In it Hartmann stated that he knew "from the first week of my arrival" that Mme. Blavatsky "was a trickster," and that, "She is worse than you think and she lied to me about lots of things." Olcott had convinced himself that the letter was a forgery, with which conclusion Hartmann was happy to concur (he called it "nonsensical" but admitted that it was "a tolerably good imitation of my own handwriting").

Whatever the truth about this letter, and all of the phenomena at Adyar, there was clearly an unhappy situation among the theosophists. Hartmann developed a great personal dislike for Dâmodar Mavalankar (H.P.B.'s most active Hindu disciple), and accused him of being a liar and the forger of some of the Mahatma letters. He also felt that Madame Blavtasky did sometimes resort to trickery, but excused her by espousing the pernicious doctrine of the end—"to induce the people to study the higher laws of life, to raise them up to a higher conception of eternal truth"—justifying the means. After all the uproar surrounding the Coulomb affair, Hartmann was happy to return to Europe with H.P.B. and her party of theosophists. They set sail on April 1, 1885.

In December of that year, after a stay in Italy, the travellers reached Germany. H.P.B. went to Wurzburg while Hartmann visited his family at Kempten. He remained in Germany but regularly visited Madame Blavastky in Wurzburg, and later in London. Despite their mutual misgivings, they remained on friendly terms and Hartmann wrote a long essay, "H.P. Blavatsky and her Mission," for the memorial volume published after her death in 1891. By this time he had become a significant figure in theosophical circles: much published—with ten books to his name—and respected, if not personally liked. But he had also "become tired of 'theosophy'" and decided to return to America. Then came another turning point in his life.

Hartmann never lost his cautious respect for H.P.B. and he did not allow his private opinions to influence his German translation of *The Secret Doctrine* (1899). His own books, however, all show his gradual drift back to the Western Hermetic Tradition. From *Magic White and Black* (1886), through his two Rosicrucian studies, his novels, his work on geomancy, to his lives of Paracelsus, Jesus, and Jacob Boehme (1891), the Western slant is pronounced—as it is in all of his subsequent works. And, perhaps unconsciously, Hartmann was seeking a Western teacher, whom he duly found at Kempten. He never revealed this man's name, describing him simply as "an occultist who was the leader of a small body of real Rosicrucians," but he exercised a profound influence over Hartmann.

These self-effacing Rosicrucians, who "wished to remain unknown and avoided publicity" and whose two leaders "were not even able to read and write," were mostly weavers at a local factory. Hartmann attended their meetings, became a disciple of the unnamed occultist and "followed his instructions for many years." There did not seem to be any set course of instruction and the teaching of these Rosicrucians consisted of:

> showing the way to the direct perception of truth and preparing oneself to receive this revelation within . . . they asked questions on which one had to meditate and find the answer oneself, and the guidance took place not so much by any external means or verbal advice, as by symbolic visions seen during dreams or in a state of meditation.

The probable source of these teachings, which presumably came to them by verbal instruction, seems to have been the philosophy of Jacob Boehme, supplemented by the symbolic images of the Behmenist tradition.

Hartmann stated publicly that "many of the truths contained in the numerous books which I have written were made clear to me by [the Rosicrucian's] guidance."

If this was so, then Hartmann must have met him long before H.P.B. died, and it is thus Rosicrucian rather than neo-theosophical teaching that permeates his writing. It has to be admitted, however, that the theory of occultism set out in *With the Adepts* still owes much to standard theosophical teaching, despite its setting "among the Rosicrucians."

In some ways the novel is reminiscent of *Lost Horizon*, although it sets out to educate rather than to enthrall. There is the same population of enigmatic figures in an inaccessible monastery, the same religious syncretism, sensual temptations, and the price to be paid by giving in to them. But while *Lost Horizon* is wholly fiction, one significant feature in *With the Adepts* is not: the "precious book" that the narrator finds, *The Secret Symbols of the Rosicrucians*, was real. Hartmann himself had published it.

The *Geheime Figuren der Rosenkreuzer aus dem 16ten und 17ten Jahrhundert*, to give its original title, first appeared at Altona, in northern Germany, in 1785-1788. Hartmann produced the first English translation, complete with color plates, in 1888. He retitled it *Cosmology, or Universal Science*, and claimed to have translated it from "an old German manuscript." Although this was possibly true, for there are manuscript copies of the text and he did examine Julius Sachse's D.O.M.A. manuscript, he is more likely to have worked from a printed copy. Much of the original material is omitted from Hartmann's translation, for which he was roundly condemned by Manly Palmer Hall, who also criticized errors in the translation and the inclusion of additional text written by Hartmann. But publication of the book did bring it within the reach of many who marvelled at (and benefitted from) its symbolic images, which constitute a remarkable series of Western mandalas.

Such symbols had previously been confined to very restricted groups, among them the Rosicrucians of Kempten, Behmenist circles in England, and the Shakers in America. What spiritual current brought a knowledge of these images to the Shakers is not known, but their "Gift Drawings"—records of spirit visions, made in watercolours and ink, in the 1850s—bear a startling resemblance to Behmenist and Rosicrucian designs. It is possible that Hartmann had visited both Shaker colonies and the German Pietists of Pennsylvania, who were the source of Sachse's Rosicrucian manuscript, but he has left no record of any such visit and it is now impossible to know whether he found his copy of the "Secret Symbols" in Germany or the United States.

But however diverse the sources of Hartmann's Rosicrucian knowledge were, their influence upon him was powerful. It was tempered by a recognition on his part that as the theosophists published his books, so he had to maintain at least a semblance of theosophical content. This led to some curious contradictions between titles and texts, as with the Appendix to *In the Pronaos of the Temple of Wisdom* (1890). It is titled "The Principles of the Yoga—Philosophy of the Rosicrucians and Alchemists," and yet it contains absolutely nothing that can be remotely connected to yoga. But it kept the Theosophical Publishing Society happy.

Despite his disenchantment with the Theosophical Society, Hartmann edited the German theosophical journal *Lotusblüthen* from 1893 to 1900. When the society split in 1895, Hartmann followed W.Q. Judge's faction, and was for a brief period in 1897 President of the German Section under Judge's successor, Katharine Tingley. Later in that year he founded a theosophical group of his own, and in 1899 took under his wing Hugo Vollrath, who would become an important publisher of occult literature—and a thorn in the flesh of Rudolf Steiner. While all this was going on, Hartmann branched out in another new direction, this time in the field of medicine.

He was now moving in German occult circles outside the Theosophical Society and in 1896 met Karl Kellner, an industrial chemist involved in paper-making. Kellner was very much a practical occultist and heavily involved with a variety of quasi-masonic orders. He was also much impressed with Hartmann, whom he saw as a high initiate and true Rosicrucian. More than this he provided Hartmann with a new career: in 1899 Kellner appointed him as director of the Lahmann Sanatorium at Hallein in Austria. Here, among the mountains which he firmly believed were inhabited by gnomes, Hartmann applied Kellner's "Ligno-Sulphite Inhalation Treatment" to patients suffering from tubercolosis. In addition to his medical activities he began to involve himself in esoteric orders.

Through Kellner, Hartmann had come to know Theodor Reuss, who in 1902 appointed him as Grand Administrator General in the newly formed Sovereign Sanctuary of the German version of the Antient and Primitive Rite of Memphis and Misraim. Although Hartmann was not and never had been a Freemason, he was immediately promoted to the office of Deputy Grand Commander General. After Kellner's death in 1905, Hartmann became Honorary Grand Master General of the Rite, but it fell apart shortly afterwards and he took no part in its later incarnations.

For the remaining seven years of his life, Hartmann devoted himself to his writing. Most of this later work appeared only in German, but between 1906 and his death, on August 7, 1912, he was a regular contributor to *The Occult Review*, supplying twenty-three articles on a wide range of esoteric topics, and drawing heavily on his own experiences. In the course of these articles he provided also an insight into his own beliefs and theories—some of which are not easy to accept, while others display both tolerance and a refreshing breath of commonsense.

Hartmann had grown up in the Roman Catholic faith, and although he came to reject its doctrines and dogmas, he retained a love for its ceremonies, knowing that "behind all this outward show and ceremony there must be some mysterious, living influence or power."

His religion was neither Christian nor neo-Buddhist, but one of Universal Love—a recognition of man's own divine, universal Self. And this is the true nature of the theosophical "Masters," not advanced supermen, but our own higher selves. Hartmann believed that "everybody has such a light hidden within his own soul; but not everybody is conscious of it." In the same vein he argued that "true religion is the realisation of Truth. The Truth can only be one and never changes, and as we change, so our aspect of the Truth changes with us."

He did not believe that asceticism was a necessary part of spirituality. For him, "to become spiritual physical health, intellectual growth and spiritual activity should go hand in hand. Intuition should be supported by an unselfish intellect, a pure mind by a healthy form." In essence this is the message of *With the Adepts*. It is buried in very Victorian prose, but the story still has the power to fascinate as well as to instruct us. Franz Hartmann was a firm believer in human reincarnation, and whatever our own belief in the matter may be we can all agree that his book deserves another lease of life.

—R. A. Gilbert

WITH THE ADEPTS

I

THE EXCURSION

I AM penning these lines in a little village in the Alpine mountains, in Southern Bavaria, and only a short distance from the Austrian frontier. The impressions I received yesterday are still fresh in my mind; the experiences which caused them were as real to me as any other experience caused by the events of every-day life; nevertheless, they were of such an extraordinary character that I cannot persuade myself that they were more than a dream.

Having finished the long and tedious labour of investigating the history of the Rosicrucians, and studying old worm-eaten books, mouldy manuscripts hardly legible from age, passing days and parts of night in convent libraries and antiquarian shops, collecting and copying everything that seemed to be of any value for my object in view, and having at last finished my task, I made up my mind to grant to myself

A

a few holidays, and to spend them among the sublime scenery of the Tyrolian Alps.

The mountains were not yet free from snow, although the spring had advanced; but I was anxious to escape the turmoil and noise of the city, to breathe once more the pure and exhilarating air of the mountain heights, to see the shining glaciers glistening like vast mirrors in the light of the rising sun, and to share the feeling of the poet Byron when he wrote the following verses :—

" He who ascends to mountain tops shall find
    The loftiest peaks most wrapp'd in clouds and snow ;
He who surpasses or subdues mankind
    Must look down on the hate of those below ;
    Though high *above* the sun of glory glow,
And far *beneath* the earth and ocean spread,
    Round him are icy rocks, and loudly blow
Contending tempests on his naked head,
And thus reward the toils which to these summits led."

Boarding the train, I soon arrived at the foot of the hills. Thence I wandered on foot, highly enjoying the change from the smoky atmosphere of the crowded streets to the fresh air of the country, pregnant with the odour of the pines and the daisies, the latter of which were appearing in places from which the snow was gone. The road led up through the valley of the river, and, as I advanced, the valley grew narrower and the sides of the mountain steeper. Here and there were clusters of farmhouses, and some rustic cottages clinging to the projecting rocks of the mountains as if seeking protection against the storms which often blow through these valleys. The sun was sinking down below the western horizon, and gilded the snowy peaks of the mountains and the brazen cross on the top of the spire of the little village church, from which tolled the curfew, or, as it is here called, the *Ave Maria,* when I arrived at the place selected as a starting-point for my excursions into the mountains.

Finding a hospitable reception in the village inn, I soon retired to rest, and awoke early in the morning, having been aroused from my sleep by the tinkling of little bells hanging around the necks of the goats which were sent out to their pasturage. I arose and stepped to the window. The shadows of night were fleeing before the approach of the coming sun; the dawn had begun, and before me in sublime array stood the grand old peaks of the mountains, reminding me of Edwin Arnold's description of the view to be had from the windows of Prince Siddârtha's palace, Vishramvan. There the grand mountains stood—

"Ranged in white ranks against the blue-untrod
  Infinite, wonderful—whose uplands vast,
  And lifted universe of crest and crag,
  Shoulder and shelf, green slope and icy horn,
  Riven ravine and splintered precipice,
  Led climbing thought higher and higher, until
  It seemed to stand in heaven and speak with gods."

Soon I was on the way, and wandered farther up through the valley along the river-bed; but the river was here merely a small stream, rushing and dancing wildly over the rocks, while farther down, where it had grown big, it flowed in tranquil majesty through the plains. The valley through which I wandered seemed to cut through long ranges of mountains, and other valleys opened into this. Some of these valleys were known to me, for I had roamed through them and explored their mysterious recesses, caves, and forests some twenty years ago; but there was one mysterious valley which had not yet been explored by me, and which led towards a high, bifurcated mountain peak, whose summit was said to be inaccessible, and upon which the foot of no mortal had ever trod. Towards this valley I seemed to be attracted by some invisible but irresistible power. I felt as if, in its unexplored depths at the foot of this inaccessible mountain, the secret and undefined longings of my heart were to be satisfied; as if there a mystery was to be revealed to me, whose solution could not be found in books.

The sun had not yet risen above the horizon, and the dark woods to the right and left were of a uniform colour. As I entered the narrow, mysterious valley, the path rose gradually, leading through a dark forest along the side

of a mountain. Slowly and almost impercep-
tibly it ascended; at first it was near the rushing
stream, but as I progressed the roar of the
torrent sounded more and more distant; the
foaming stream itself seemed to sink farther
down. At last the forest became thinner, and
the dark woods were now far below me; but
before me and above the intervening trees rose
the naked cliffs of the inaccessible mountain.
Still the path led up higher. Soon the distant
noise of a waterfall was heard, and I approached
again the bed of the mountain stream, which,
however, now seemed to be a mass of rocks,
split into pieces by some giant power, lying
about in wild confusion, while the white foam
of the water danced between the cliffs.

Here and there were little islands of soil
covered with green vegetation. They stood
like isolated tables in the midst of the wilder-
ness; for the combined action of water and air
had decomposed and eaten away a great part of
their foundations, and they looked like plates of
soil resting upon small pedestals; hard as they
are, their final tumble is merely a question of
time, for their foundations are slowly crumbling
away.

My path took me upwards, sometimes nearing
the river-bed, sometimes receding from it, leading
sometimes over steep rocks, and again descending

to the bottom of ravines formed by the melting snows. Thus I entered deep into the mysterious valley, when the first signs of sunrise appeared upon the cliffs above my head. One of these towering peaks was crowned with a halo of light, while beyond it the full sunlight streamed into the valley below. A mild breeze swept through the tops of the trees, and the foliage of the birch-trees, with which the pine forest was sprinkled, trembled in the morning air. No sound could now be heard, except occasionally the note of a titmouse, and more rarely the cry of a hawk which rose in long-drawn, spiral motions high up into the air to begin its work of the day.

Now the ash-gray walls and cliffs began to assume a pale silvery hue, while in the rents and crags of the rock the dark blue shade seemed to resist the influence of the light. Looking backwards, I saw how the valley widened, and, far down, the stream could be seen as it wandered towards the plains. Obtaining more room as it advanced, it spread, and formed ponds and tanks and little lakes among the meadows. On the opposite side of the valley rose the tops of high mountains far into the sky, and between the interstices of the summits, still more summits arose. The foot of the range was covered with a dark vegetation, but the mountain sides exhibited a great variety of colours, from the almost black appearance of the rocks below to the ethereal white of the farthest peaks, whose delicate hues seemed to blend with the pale blue sky. Here and there the surface was already covered with spots of light from the rising sun, falling through the rents of the rocks and through the branches of trees, foreboding the near arrival of the orb of day. Thus the higher peaks enjoyed the warm light of the sun long before it shone into the valley below; but while it shone in its full brightness upon the mountain tops, the dark shadows in the deep valley became thinner and began to disappear.

At last the solemn moment arrived, and the sun rose in his sublime majesty over the tops of the mountains, becoming visible to all. The shadows fled, and a flood of light penetrated into the valley, lightening up the dark forest of pines and illuminating the caves of the rocks. Shining upon the fields of snow and the glaciers, its light was reflected as in a mirror and produced a blinding effect, but upon the rocky surface it became softened, and gave it the appearance of a thousand various hues.

The road turned round a projecting part of the height, and suddenly I stood in full view of the inaccessible mountain. Between the place where I stood and the base of the mountain

there was a well-nigh treeless plain, and the soil
was almost without any vegetation. Everywhere the ground was covered with stones and
rocks, many of which seemed to have fallen
down from the mysterious mountain and to have
been broken in the fall. Here and there was
a small spot covered with moss or small vegetation, sending fantastically-shaped branches of
green upwards along the sides of the inaccessible
mountain towards the bare gray walls of the
summit, where giant sentinels of a forbidding
mien stood eternal and immovable, and seemed
to defend their strongholds against the aggressive
vegetation, crowding the latter back into the
valley. Thus the everlasting combat which
had been raging for untold ages still continued;
but the front lines of the contending armies
changed from year to year. Everlasting, like
the eternal truths, stand the bare gray rocks
upon the summits; here and there the vegetation
invades their kingdom, like illusions approaching
the realm of the real; death is victorious; the
green spots are buried each year under the
descending rocks; but again life is the victor,
for those rocks decay, and a new life appears
upon their withered faces.

In the limestone formation of the Alpine
ranges, the rocks decomposed by wind and
rain assume often the most fantastic shapes,

which suggest the names which are given to the mountains. Very little power of imagination is required to behold in the shape of the summits of the Wilden Kaiser mountain the figure of the Emperor Barbarossa, with his long red beard, with crown and sceptre, lying in state, unaffected by the cold of the winter or the summer's heat, waiting to be resurrected ; or we may see in the shape of the Hochvogel the form of an eagle spreading its wings ; in the Widderhorn, the shape of the horns of a ram, &c. At the base of the mountains and in the valleys the soil is covered with small loose rocks and piles of sand, in the midst of which the coltsfoot plant (*Tussilago farfara*) spreads its large green leaves, and the blue bell-shaped flowers of the monkshood (*Aconitum napellus*) wave their heads. In some secluded spots grows the celebrated edelweiss (*Gnaphalium leontopodium*), resembling in size those which grow on the Popocatepetl in Mexico, and on the Cordilleras of South America. There may also be found the mountain gentian, the Alpine rose, the mandrake, *Arnica montana*, the mysterious *Hypericon*, and other curious plants full of healing powers and strange virtues. Wherever a sufficient quantity of soil has accumulated to enable a tree to grow, a larger kind of vegetation appears ; but the little crust of earth is not deep enough to afford a solid footing to large trees. They may grow to a certain height, but some day a storm will arise and sweep down the mountain sides, and then the work of destruction begins. Grand old tree-corpses, whose roots have been torn from the soil, are lying about, their barkless, bleached branches like so many skeleton arms stretched up towards heaven, as if they had been calling for help in the hour of their death, but no help had arrived. Smaller growths of dwarf-trees surround them, and cover the ground or feed like parasites upon the substance of the dead.

The spring had advanced; but among these mountains the seasons are interlaced with each other. The red and yellow leaves painted by autumn were seen among the green foliage of the stunted pines. The moss clinging to the steep precipices shows the reddish colour obtained in the fall, and in many clefts and caverns linger the snow and ice of the past winter; but above the red and green and the pure white snow the gray masses of the summits rise in a succession of pillars and points, with domes and spires and pinnacles, like a city built by the gods; while in the background spreads the gray or blue canopy of heaven. Thin streams of water run down from these heights over the precipices, and as they splash over the projecting rocks they are reduced to vapour before reaching the ground below. The rocks themselves have been hollowed out, forming large caves, and indicating how powerful those little veins of water may become, if swelled by the floods from the melting snows of the summits.

After enjoying for a few minutes the sublimity of this scenery, I continued my way and approached a little stream coming from a waterfall in the distance. I wandered along its border; the water was deep, but so clear that even the smallest pebble could be distinctly seen at the bottom. Sometimes it appeared as motionless as if it were liquid crystal penetrated by the rays of the sun, and again, meeting with obstacles in its way, it foamed in its rocky bed as if in a sudden fit of rage, while in other places it tumbled in little cascades over pretty pebbles and stones, forming miniature cataracts which exhibited manifold colours.

In these solitudes there is nothing to remind one of the existence of man, except occasionally the sawn-off trunk of a tree, showing the destructive influence of human activity. In some old, rotten, and hollow trunks rain-water has collected, sparkling in the sun like little mirrors, such as may be used by water nymphs, and around their edges little mushrooms are growing, which our imagination transforms into chairs, tables, and baldachinos for fairies and elves.

Where I now stood, the ground was covered with moss, and occasionally there was to be seen a great, white thistle, whose sharp-pointed leaves sparkled in the sunlight. At a short distance I saw a small grove of pines, looking like an island in the desert, and to that grove I directed my steps. There I resolved to rest and enjoy the beauty of nature. I laid myself down upon the moss in a place which was overshadowed by a mighty pine. The music of the mountain stream was heard at a distance, and opposite to the place where I rested there was to be seen a waterfall, spreading into a vapour as it fell over the rocks, and in the vapour appeared the colours of the rainbow. The mist fell into a basin formed of rock, and from a rent in this basin, overgrown with moss, the water foamed and rushed, hastening down towards the valley, to become united with the main body of the river.

For a long time I watched the play of the water, and the longer I watched the more did it become alive with forms of the most singular shape. Supermundane beings of great beauty seemed to dance in the spray, shaking their heads in the sunshine and throwing showers of liquid silver from their streaming curls and

waving locks. Their laughter sounded like that
of the falls of Minnehaha, and from the crevices
of the rocks peeped the ugly faces of gnomes
and kobolds watching slyly the dance of the
fairies. Above the fall the current seemed to
hesitate before throwing itself down over the
precipice; but below, where it left the basin,
it appeared to be irritated by the impediments
in its way and impatient to leave its home;
while far down in the valley, where it became
united to its brother, the river, it sounded as if
the latter was welcoming it back to its bosom,
and as if both were exulting over their final
union in a glad jubilee.

What is the reason that we imagine such
things? Why do we endow "dead things"
with human consciousness and with sensation?
Why are we in our moments of happiness not
satisfied to feel that we live in a body, but our
consciousness craves to go out of its prison-
house and mix with the universal life? Is our
consciousness merely a product of the organic
activity of our physical body, or is it a function
of the universal life, concentrated—so to say—
in a focus within the physical body? Is our
personal consciousness dependent for its existence on the existence of the physical body, and
does it die with the latter; or is there a spiritual
consciousness, belonging to a higher, immortal,

and invisible self of man, which is temporarily connected with the physical organism, but which may exist independent of the latter? If such is the case, if our physical organism is merely an instrument through which our consciousness acts, then this instrument is not our real self. If this is true, then our real self may exist independently of the latter. If we mentally float along the curves of the mountain tops, sinking gradually downwards, rising suddenly upwards, and examining in our imagination the things upon their surface, why do we feel such a sense of exhilaration and joy, as if we were really there, but had left our material body behind, because too heavy to accompany the spirit to the top of the inaccessible mountain? It is true, a part of our life and consciousness must remain with the physical form, to enable it to continue to live during our absence and to attend to the functions of life; but we have read of somnambules and persons in an ecstatic condition, whose inner spiritual self, with all its powers of consciousness, sensation, and perception, was absent from their apparently dead forms, and who visited distant places, going and returning with the velocity of thought, and bringing descriptions of such places which were afterwards verified and found to be true.

Why do we find life in all things, even in those which are considered "dead," if we merely put ourselves in a condition in which we can perceive that they are living? Can there be any dead matter in the universe? Is not even a stone held together by the "cohesion" of its particles, and attracted to the earth by "gravitation"? But what else is this "cohesion" and "gravitation" but *energy*, and what is "energy" but the *Soul*, an interior principle called *force*, which produces an outward manifestation called *matter*; but which must ultimately be identical with force or substance, or by whatever name we may call a thing of which we have no conception. If this view is correct, then all things possess life, all things possess soul, and there may be soul-beings, whose outward forms are not so gross as ours, and who are therefore invisible to our physical senses, but may be perceived by our own soul.

In the silence of nature thoughts grow to be waking dreams, and dreams become visions. I imagined how in this solemn solitude I might remain all the rest of my life, perhaps sharing my habitation with a few congenial friends. I imagined how, united by common interests and having identical objects in view, we might be happy and obtain knowledge together. Here, far away from the superficiality and shallowness of common life, a far greater clearness of mental perception, a much deeper concentration of thought, a much higher conception of the truth regarding the mysteries of nature and man might be obtained.   How much would our senses be sharpened for the perception of external and internal things ! how much would our knowledge of self increase !   What should we care about the tomfooleries of what is called "society"; what should we care to know of what is going on in that great insane asylum called "the world" ? Here we could live undisturbed within our own selves, unpestered by the necromantic practices of "society," which daily and hourly force us to go out from within our own selves, to appear where we do not desire to be, compel us to act as we do not desire to act, to bow down before the goddess of fashion, whom we despise in our hearts.

Would such a life be useful for us and useful for others ?   If it is true that the world and we ourselves are made up of ideas, then it is just in such solitudes that the best conditions might be found in which to grasp and remodel ideas.   Thoughts and ideas cannot be merely illusions ; they must have a real existence, as real and perhaps more lasting than the objective things of this world ; for we know that ideas outlive the death of the forms in which they are represented ; we know that ideas, like other fruits, are born and become mature, and whenever an idea is mature it appears on the mental horizon of the world, and is often grasped at the same time by some receptive minds. A man who is able to grasp and remodel exalted ideas, and give them material expression, may do much more for the benefit of the world by living alone and in solitude, than by living among the world where his work is continually impeded by affairs of minor importance. The ideas which he shapes will not die with his body. They will be thrown upon the great mirror, the Astral Light, and be preserved in the memory of the world, to be grasped and utilised by others.

What is that being we call *man*, after all? What is this living animal organism of flesh, blood, and bones, nerves and mind, which lives for a while and then dies, and which the great majority of people esteem so highly, as if it were their own immortal self, and for the comfort of which they often sacrifice their self-respect, their dignity, honour, and virtue? Is it anything else than an animal in whom an intellectual activity of a higher order than in other animals predominates? Can this mental activity be the product of the mechanical, chemical, and physiological activity of gross matter? If not, what is the cause of this activity, and can this cause exist independently of the form? What is a man without any intelligence ? If intelligence, as it necessarily must be, is an attribute of the spirit, what is a man without any spirit and without spiritual intelligence ?

While I was meditating about this question a stupid laughter sounded close by my side. I had been so much engaged with my own thoughts that I had not noticed the approach of the stranger ; but looking up I saw close by my side one of those half-idiotic human beings whom they call *cretins*, and who are often found in the mountainous countries of Switzerland and Savoy. I was somewhat surprised and startled, and not a little annoyed at the unwelcome interruption, and I asked him rather abruptly, " What do you want ? "

A broad grin passed over the face of the dwarf, for such he certainly was, as he answered, " Master says I should guide you to his house." I was somewhat astonished by his reply, but remembering that the dwarf was an idiot, and that no intelligent answer was to be expected from him, I asked, " Who is your master ? " His answer was, " Imperator "; and as he spoke that word a spark of intelligence seemed to shine in his eyes, and the tone of his voice seemed to indicate that this Imperator, whoever he might be, was undoubtedly somebody to whom the cretin rendered implicit obedience. I attempted to ask the dwarf more questions, and to find out who his Imperator was, or where he lived, but all my efforts to obtain information from one who was evidently an idiot were unavailing, and he merely grinned and repeated the words which he had already said before. I therefore at last made up my mind to go with him and see how the adventure would end.

The cretin walked ahead and I followed him; he led me towards the base of the inaccessible mountain. While we were walking on, and the idiot often turned back to see whether I was following him, I had a good opportunity to study his dress and features. He was not over three feet high, and evidently a hunchback. His clothing consisted of a brown gown, to which a hood was attached, which made him appear like a small Capuchin monk of the order of St. Augustine. An immense big head and a comparatively large body rested upon very thin and small legs, while his feet seemed again to be extraordinarily large. Perhaps on account of his small size and the healthy colour of his face, he appeared to be almost a child; but this opinion was contradicted by a gray beard of considerable length which adorned his face. In his hand he carried a staff made of a dead limb of a tree, which he had evidently picked up on his way.

II

THE MONASTERY

I FOLLOWED my weird companion, and soon we regained the path running along the bed of the creek, which flowed tranquilly over a bottom covered with white pebbles, and the shallowness of the water seemed to indicate that we were not far from its source. As we approached the mysterious mountain the stone walls appeared to rise perpendicularly before us, and there was no place visible where any other being but a bird could have ascended; but as we came still nearer, I noticed a rent or break in the side of the wall, opening like a cave or a tunnel. This tunnel we entered, and, as we proceeded, I saw that it penetrated the giant wall and led into another valley beyond. We arrived at the other end of the tunnel, and an exclamation of joy and surprise escaped my lips as I beheld the beautiful sight which presented itself to my view.

Before me was a valley surrounded by mountains of evidently inaccessible height, and this

valley nature and art seemed to have combined to endow with an almost superterrestrial beauty. Like a vast ocean bay it opened
before my sight, closing in the distance with a
kind of natural amphitheatre. It was covered
with short grass and planted with maple trees,
and on all sides there were forests and groves,
small lakes and lovely creeks. Immediately in
front of me, but still at a considerable distance,
rose the vault of a sublime mountain peak high
into the blue ether of space, presenting a cavity
with overhanging rocks, looking like the hollow
space under a gigantic wave, which had been
petrified by some magic spell. The sides of
the mountain sank sheer towards a lower de-
clivity, and then again rose abruptly to an
imposing height.

In the presence of so much sublimity I became
dumfounded. My companion seemed to comprehend my feeling ; for he, too, stood still and
laughed, as if he were pleased to see how full
of admiration I was. The stillness which surrounded us would have been complete if it had
not been for the noise of a cataract, at a distance
to the left, falling over a steep precipice and
appearing like a string of fluid silver backed by
the dark gray rock. The monotonous rush of
that fall in contradistinction to the surrounding
stillness seemed to me like the rush of the river

of time in the realm of eternity; another world
than the one to which I had been accustomed
seemed to have descended upon me; the air
seemed more pure, the light more ethereal, the
grass more green than on the other side of the
tunnel; here seemed to be the valley of peace,
the paradise of happiness and content.

Looking towards the high peak in the distance, I noticed what seemed to be a palace, a
fortress, or a monastery of some kind, and as I
came nearer, I saw it was a massive building of
stone. Its high walls rose above the tops of
the surrounding trees, and a dome, as if of a
temple, crowned the top of the building. Its
exterior appearance indicated the solidity of the
walls. It was built in rectangular form, but
its architecture was not of a regular style; it
presented many projecting windows, turrets,
balconies, and verandas.

On the other side of the valley nature was
not less sublime and inspiring. Gray giant cliffs,
standing out prominently against the steel-blue
background of the sky, rose up to an extraordinary height. Below the highest peaks long
strips of white clouds had settled around the
mountain, and seemed to separate the top of
the latter from its main body. The part below
the cloud was partly covered by the shadow
and partly illuminated by a pale ghostly light,

producing a glamour. There, where the masses of clouds rested against the bulk of the mountain, it seemed to me that I was looking into a world of destruction. It was as if the entrails of the mountain had been torn up, and the uniformity of the desolate jumble of rocks was only interrupted by a few remnants of snow situated in the caverns and on the crags of the mountain.

As we advanced we came into a broad avenue leading to the building, and I beheld a man of noble and imposing appearance approaching. He was clad in a yellow robe, his head covered with black flowing hair, and he walked with an elastic step. When the cretin saw this man he hurried towards him, prostrated himself before him, and suddenly vanished, like an image of a dream.

I was struck with astonishment by this extraordinary occurrence, but I had no time to reflect, for the stranger approached me and bid me welcome. He appeared to be a man of about thirty-five years of age, of tall and commanding stature; and his mild and benevolent look, full of spiritual energy, seemed to penetrate my whole being and to read my innermost thoughts. "Surely," I thought, "this man is an Adept!"

"Yes," answered the stranger, as if he had been reading my thought, "you have fallen into the hands of the Adepts, of whom you have thought so much and whose acquaintance you often desired to make, and I will introduce you into our temple and make you acquainted with some of our *Brothers of the Golden and Rosy Cross.*"

I scanned his face, and now it seemed to me as if this man were not a stranger to me. There was something so familiar about him, as if I had known him for years, and yet I could not find a place for him in my memory. In vain I tortured my brain to find out when or where I had met this man, or at least some other one resembling him in appearance. But again the Imperator of this "Rosicrucian Society," for such he proved to be, answered my unspoken thought by saying: "You are right; we are not strangers, for I have often been in your presence and stood by your side, although you did not see me. I have directed the flow of ideas which streamed into your brain, while you elaborated them and put them down in writing. Moreover, this place has often been visited by you while your animal body was sleeping, and you have conversed with me and with the brothers; but when your soul returned to its house of flesh and blood, it could not impress the memory of the brain with the recollection of the events through which you had passed, and you could remember none of your transcendental experiences when you awoke. The memory of the animal form retains only the impressions which are made upon it by the avenues of the external senses; the memory of the spirit awakens when we are in the spiritual state."

I told the Imperator that I considered this day the happiest one in my life, and only regretted that I should not be permitted to remain here for ever, as I felt that I was not yet worthy to remain in the society of beings so far exalted above my own state.

"We shall not permit you to go away very soon," answered the Master. "You will have ample time to see how we live. But as to your permanently remaining here, this is at present an impossibility. You have other duties to perform, and, moreover, there are still too many of the lower and animal elements adhering to your constitution and forming a part of yourself. They could not resist long the destructive influence of the pure and spiritual air of this place; and as you have not yet a sufficient amount of truly spiritual elements in your organism to render it firm and strong, you would, by remaining here, soon become weak and waste away like a person in a state of consumption; you would become miserable instead of being happy. You would die."

"Master," I said, "then I can at least hope to learn, while I am here, the mystery of those great spiritual powers which you possess; by which you are said to be able to transform one thing into another, and transmute base metals into gold?"

"There is nothing mysterious or wonderful about it, my friend," said the Imperator. "Such things are not more wonderful than the ordinary phenomena of nature which we see every day. They are only mysterious to those whose own prejudices and misconceptions hinder them from seeing the truth and knowing the power the spirit possesses to subjugate matter by means of the soul. We need not be surprised about them any more than about seeing the moon revolve around the earth, or watching the growth of a tree. It is all merely the effect of that one primordial power which is called the Will, and which called the world into existence. It manifests itself in various ways as mechanical force or as a spiritual power; but it is always the same divine power of Will, acting through the instrumentality of the organism of man, who directs it by his intelligence."

"Then," I said, "the principal requirement

would be to learn how to strengthen the Will?"

"Not so," said the Imperator. "The Will is the law, the universal power holding together the worlds in space and causing the revolutions of planets; it pervades and penetrates everything, and does not require your strengthening it, for it is already strong enough to accomplish everything. You are only an instrument through which this spiritual power may act and manifest itself, if you do not attempt to oppose it."

"Then," I said, "how can we accomplish anything at all? If we can do nothing through the power of our own will, we may as well never attempt to do anything."

"We can accomplish nothing useful," answered the Master, "by attempting to employ any separate will of our own; but we may employ our Reason and Intelligence to guide and conduct the already existing universal Will-power in Nature which constitutes the life of all things, and thus we may accomplish in a few moments certain things which it would require unconscious nature much longer periods of time to accomplish without our aid. The miller who employs the water of a river to set his mill in motion does not create water, nor does he attempt to make the river run upwards towards its source; he merely leads the stream into certain channels and uses the already existing current in an intelligent manner to accomplish his purpose. He knows the law of nature and acts in accordance with it. Being obedient to that law he is able to employ it. Nature obeys those who act in obedience to her laws. In the same manner acts the Adept. He guides the existing spiritual power by his intelligence, and thereby causes it to accomplish certain things in accordance with the law of nature."

"Do you see yonder cloud which has settled below the top of the mountain?" continued the Adept. "It will remain there until some current of air blows it away, or until a change of temperature causes it to rise or to fall. If we disperse it by causing the universal forces of nature to act upon the dense masses, we do not act against the law of nature, but guide it by our intelligence."

While the Master spoke these words, he extended his hands toward the mountain, below whose top the clouds had collected, and immediately it seemed as if life had been infused into the dense mass. It began to whirl and to dance, and finally it rose like a column of smoke up to the top of the mountain, ascending from there high up into the air, giving the mountain the appearance of a volcano. At last it collected again far above the top, in the air, forming a little silvery cloud, through which the sunshine was streaming.

I wondered at this manifestation of life in a cloud; but the Adept, reading my thoughts, said: "Life is universal and everywhere; it is identical with the Will."

During our conversation we had slowly approached the building, and I had now an opportunity to examine its exterior in all its details. It was only two stories high, but the rooms seemed to be lofty. It was built in a quadrangular form, and surrounded by oaks and maple trees, and a large garden or park. Seven steps of white marble led up to the main portal, which was protected by two massive pillars of granite, and over the door appeared in golden letters an inscription, saying: *You, who enter here, leave all evil thoughts behind.*

We entered through the portal into a large vestibule paved with flagstones. In the midst of this room was a statue of Gautama Buddha on a pedestal, and the walls were ornamented with golden inscriptions representing some of the most important doctrines of the ancient sages. To the right and left, doors opened into long corridors leading to the various apartments of the Brothers; but the door opposite the entrance led into a beautiful garden, where I beheld many plants and trees such as are usually only to be found in tropical climes. The back of this garden was formed by a building of white marble, surrounded by the dome which I had seen from the distance, after entering through the tunnel, and on the top of the dome was a silver dragon resting on a golden globe.

"This," said the Imperator, "is the sanctuary of our temple; in this you cannot enter. If you were to attempt it, the immediate death of your personality would be the consequence; nor would it serve you even if you were able to enter and live, for in that sanctuary everything is dark to all who do not bring with them their own spiritual light, the inextinguishable lamp of divine intelligence, to illuminate the darkness."

We walked into one of the corridors. On our left there were numerous doors leading into the cells or apartments of the Brothers, but to the right was a wall, occasionally opening into the tropical garden, and the interstices between these openings were filled out with beautifully painted landscapes. One of these landscapes represented Indian scenery, with the white snow-covered Himalaya Mountains in the background, while the fore-part of the picture represented what appeared to be a Chinese pagoda, with a small lake and wooded hills at a distance.

"These pictures," the Master explained, "represent the various monasteries or lamaseries of our order. The one before you is situated near a lake in the interior of *Tibet*, and is occupied by some of the highest Adepts of our order. Each of these pictures shows also a part of the country in which the monastery is placed, so as to give a correct idea of the general character of the locality. But these pictures have an occult quality which will become apparent to you if you concentrate your mind upon some part of the picture."

I did as directed, and concentrated my attention upon the grand portal of the lamasery, and to my astonishment the door opened, and the tall form of an Indian, dressed in shining white robes, with a turban of pale yellow silk upon his head, stepped out of the door. I immediately recognised him to be one of the Tibetan Adepts whom I had seen in my waking dreams. He, too, seemed to recognise me, and smilingly nodded his head, while I bowed reverentially before him. A fine-looking horse was brought forward by some attendant, and he mounted and rode away.

I was speechless from astonishment, but the Imperator smiled and drew me away, quoting a passage of Shakespeare, with a little modification ; for he said, "There are many things in

Heaven and Earth which are not understood by *your* philosophers."

We passed on to another picture, representing Egyptian scenery, with a convent in the foreground and pyramids at a distance ; it was of a more gloomy character than the former, probably on account of the desert places by which it seemed to be surrounded. The next picture represented a similar building, situated in a tropical and mountainous country, and the Adept told me it was one situated somewhere in the Cordilleras of South America. Another one showed a Mohammedan temple, with minarets and the *half-moon* upon their tops. I expressed my surprise to see all the various religious systems in the world represented in these Rosicrucian orders ; for I had always believed that the Rosicrucians were an eminently Christian order.

The Imperator, again reading my thought, corrected my mistake. " The name ' Rosicrucian Order,' or the ' Order of the Golden and Rosy Cross,' " he said, " is a comparatively modern invention, and was first used by Johann Valentin Andreæ, who invented the story of the knight Christian Rosencreuz for the same purpose as Cervantes invented his ' Don Quichote de la Mancha,' namely, for the purpose of ridiculing the would-be Adepts, reformers, and gold-makers of his age, when he wrote his celebrated 'Fama Fraternitatis.' Before his pamphlet appeared, the name Rosicrucian did not mean a person belonging to a certain organised society of that name, but it was a generic name, applied to occultists, adepts, alchemists of a higher order, in possession of some occult knowledge and acquainted with the secret signification of the *Rose* and the *Cross;* symbols which have been adopted by the Christian Church, which were, however, not invented by her, but used by occultists thousands of years before Christianity was known. These symbols do not belong exclusively to the Christian Church. They are as free as the air for any one who can grasp their meaning, but unfortunately very few of your Christians know that meaning ; they only worship the external forms, and know nothing about the principles which those forms represent."

"Then," I said, "a spiritually enlightened man may become a member of your order, even if he did not believe in any of the so-called *Christian* dogmas ? "

To this the Imperator answered : " No man can become a member of our exalted order whose knowledge is merely based upon dogmas, beliefs, creeds, or opinions which have been taught to him by somebody, or which he has accepted from hearsay or from the reading of books. Such imaginary knowledge is no *real* knowledge; we can know nothing real except that which we realise within ourselves. That which is usually called knowledge is merely a matter of memory. We may store our memory with innumerable things, and they may be true or false; but even if they are true, opinions do not convey real knowledge. Real knowledge cannot be imparted by one man to another; a man can only be guided to the place where he may obtain it; but he must himself grasp the truth, not merely intellectually with his brain, but also intuitionally with his heart.

" To obtain real knowledge we must feel the truth of a thing, and understand its true nature. To believe in the truth of anything without having real knowledge is merely a superstition. Many of your scientific, philosophical, and theological speculations are based upon superstition and not upon real knowledge or self-consciousness. The science and knowledge of your modern philosophers and theologians rest upon opinions, and are continually in danger of being overthrown by some new discovery which will not amalgamate with their artificial systems. The truth cannot be overthrown; it needs no argumentation, and if it is once perceived by the *spiritual* power of perception and understood by the *spiritual* intelligence of man, it conveys real knowledge and cannot be disputed away.

" Our order has, therefore, nothing to do with beliefs in creeds or opinions of any kind. We care nothing for them. If we were all sufficiently perfect to recognise all truths by direct perception, we should not need any books or instruments ; we should not need to use logic or make any experiments. As it is, we are still men, although far above the intellectual animal which is usually called man. We still use our books and have a library, and study the opinions of thinkers ; but we never accept such books or opinions—even if they came from Buddha himself—as our infallible guides, unless they receive the seal from our reason and understanding. We venerate them and make use of them ; they serve us, but we do not serve them."

During this conversation we walked into the library, where thousands of books were standing upon a great number of shelves. I noticed many ancient books of which I had heard, but which I had never seen. There were the sybilline books, which are said to have been destroyed by fire ; the books of Hermes Trismegistus, of which only one is believed to be in existence ; and many others of priceless value for the antiquary or the student of hermetic philosophy. While I wondered how these Brothers came into

possession of such treasures, the Imperator
said :

"Well may you be surprised how we came
into possession of books which are supposed to
exist no more ; but the secret of this is, that
everything, and consequently every book which
ever existed, leaves its imperishable impression
in the *Astral Light*, and that by certain occult
means these impressions may be reproduced
from that universal storehouse, the memory of
nature, and be put in a visible, tangible, and
material shape. Some of our Brothers are to
a great extent engaged in making such repro-
ductions, and thus we have without any finan-
cial outlay obtained these treasures, which no
amount of money could have procured."

I rejoiced to hear these words, because they
confirmed my opinion that life in a solitude
was not necessarily a life of uselessness, and
that ideas are real things, which may be seen
and grasped far more easily in a tranquil place
than while we are surrounded by the turmoil
and the petty cares of life in "society."

In answer to this thought, the Imperator said :
"Our monastery has been founded by spiritually enlightened people who had the same
thought which I read in your mind. They
therefore selected this spot in a secluded valley,
whose existence is known only to a few, and by

making use of certain elementary forces of nature, which are as yet unknown to you, they created an illusion which renders this place safe against all unwelcome intruders. Here those in whom the germ of divinity, being latent or dormant in the heart of mortal man, has awakened into life and activity, may find the conditions required for its further development. Here we live in peace, separated from the outer world by a barrier which none can surmount; for even if the existence of our retreat were known, it would be an easy matter for us to create other illusions which would prevent the intrusion of those who attempted to enter it. We are, however, not excluded from that outer world, although we seldom enter it with our physical forms. By the exercise of our clairvoyant and clairaudient powers, we may at any moment know what is going on in that world; and, if we desire to come into personal contact with it, we leave our physical forms and go out in our *astral bodies.* We visit whomsoever we wish, and witness everything without our presence being perceived. We visit the statesman, the minister, the philosopher, the inventor; we infuse thoughts in their minds which are useful, and they do not know from whence those thoughts come. If their prejudices and predilections are very strong, they may reject those thoughts; but, if they are reasonable people and know how to discriminate, they will follow the silent advice and profit by it."

"In that case," I said, "your order can exercise a tremendous influence in the politics of the world; but why, then, did you not try to abolish some of the greatest evils that afflicted the world in the history of the past? Why did you permit such monsters as Nero and Caligula to exist? Why did you permit the horrors of the Inquisition? Why did you allow the terrors of the French Revolution to take place? Why did you not destroy such villains as Louis XI of France, and others of that class?"

"Alas!" answered the Adept, "there is a certain law of justice, whose action causes evils for individuals, which we are not permitted to oppose, because its working is necessary for the evolution of the race. As the surgeon sometimes has to inflict pain for the purpose of removing a cancerous growth and saving the life of the patient, so it is often necessary to purge the organism of a nation for the purpose of restoring its health. It is said that evils are blessings in disguise, and God may execute His purpose even through instruments full of wickedness and depravity."

"Nevertheless," I interposed, "it seems to

me that you might interfere in individual cases to protect people from committing acts of imprudence which will cause them to suffer."

To this he replied : " It is true that we might handle mankind as if they were merely automata, and we could cause them to do what we please, while they would still imagine that they were following their own inclination. But to do so would be against the rules of our order and against the great Law, for the latter decides that each man shall be the creator of his own *Karma*. We are permitted to advise our followers, but we are not permitted to interfere with their mental freedom."

" Still," I persisted, " there are innocent people who have to suffer for actions not done by themselves ; there were martyrs who underwent torture and death for the sake of some great cause. Why did you not save them ? Why did you permit Hypatia to be torn to pieces by a fanatical mob, or Jeanne d'Arc to die an ignominious death upon the stake ? "

" Such people will have their reward. From the blood of a martyr springs fruit in abundance. Their bodily sufferings are as nothing in comparison with the joy they earn. Nothing is useless, although you narrow-sighted mortals cannot always see the use of a thing. Moreover, it often happens that worthy people are saved in a manner appearing to you miraculous."

A strong desire to become a member of the Rosicrucian Society entered my mind; but I did not dare to express it. The Master, however, reading my mind, continued to say:

"We accept in our circle every one who has the necessary qualifications to enter it, but you will perceive that these qualifications are not in everybody's possession; they cannot be conferred by favour, and it is a well-known saying, even among the lowest grades of occultists, that the Adept cannot be made, but that he must grow to become one."

"Master," I said, "would it not be well for those who desire to develop spiritually, and to become Adepts, to imitate your example and to select some secluded places where they could reside undisturbed and give their time to interior meditation and concentration of thought? I know that there are at present a great many people in various parts of the world, belonging to various nationalities and having various creeds, who have become convinced of the fact that the conditions, under which the majority of men and women of our present civilisation exist and live, are not conducive to the quick attainment of a higher spiritual state. They believe that the objects which people usually strive to

attain during their comparatively short life upon
this globe, such as the gratification of pride and
ambition, the hoarding of money, the enjoyment
of sexual love, the obtaining of bodily comfort
and pleasure, &c., cannot be the true objects of
life ; but that our present life is only one of the
many phases of our eternal existence, and that
terrestrial life is only a means to an end,
namely, to afford the conditions by which the
divine element, germinally contained in every
man, may grow and develop, whereby man may
attain a higher life like yours, which is not
subject to transformation and death, and is
therefore of permanent value."

The Adept, who had patiently listened to my
outburst of enthusiasm, smiled and said : " If
those people are ripe enough to be able to bear
a life of seclusion, let them enter it ; but to do
so it is above all necessary that they possess
real knowledge. As long as men move merely
on the plane of beliefs and opinion, each man's
opinions and tastes will differ from those of the
others to a certain extent, and I am afraid that
your proposed harmonial society would prove in
the end to be a very inharmonious one.

" I have, however, no doubt that even under
such unfavourable auspices considerable advantage might be derived from the establishment of
theosophical academies in secluded places. If you

had any colleges, seminaries, schools, or societies where the truth could be taught without all the accompanying rubbish of scientific and theological misconceptions and superstitions, which have accumulated through the ages, great progress would undoubtedly be made. As the present civilisation now stands, there are two methods adopted for the education of the people. One is by means of what is called *Science*, the other by means of what is called *Religion*. As far as science is concerned, her deductions and speculations are based upon observation and logic. Her logic may be good enough; but her powers of observation, upon which the fundamentals of her logic rest, are restricted to her very imperfect faculties of sensual perception, and therefore your science is based entirely upon external illusions, and is consequently a superficial and illusive science. Knowledge of the inner life of nature is far more important than the study of external phenomena.

"You must not misunderstand me," he continued, seeing that I did not fully grasp the meaning of his words. "I do not mean to say that your modern science knows nothing about natural laws. She knows what she sees and understands, but knows little or nothing about the invisible spiritual causes which are the fundamental causes of visible effects. She knows a great deal about the little details of existence which are the ultimate effects of the action of universal Life; but she knows nothing about the Tree of Life, the eternal source from which all these transient phenomena spring.

"As far as your modern theology is concerned, it is based upon an entire misconception of terms which were originally intended to signify certain spiritual powers, of which your priests and laymen can have no correct conception because they have not the spiritual powers necessary to conceive of such things. Being narrowminded, the universal principles and powers which are active within the great workshop of nature have, in their conceptions, become narrowed down to personal and limited beings; the divine universal and infinite power which men call God, has been reduced in the minds of the ignorant to an extra-cosmic deity of some kind, who can be persuaded by mortals to change His will, and who needs substitutes and deputies upon this earth to execute His divine laws. Your religion is not the religion of the living God who executes His own will; it is the religion of a dead and impotent god, who died long ago and left an army of clergymen to rule in his stead.

"Your theology should above all be based

upon the power spiritually to perceive the truth. But where can you find a clergyman who has any spiritual perceptions, and who dares to trust to his intuition more than to the dogmas prescribed by his Church? If he dared to have an opinion of his own, and to assert it, he would cease to be a minister of his Church and be considered a heretic. In your "intellectual" age everything is left to intellectual investigation alone; little is done to develop the intuitive power of the heart. The consequence is, that your present generation is like people looking at everything by means of a telescope; they may see, but they do not *feel* and grasp the truth, and the consequence is an entirely false conception of nature and man."

III

UNEXPECTED REVELATIONS

THE Adept paused, and my mind was invaded by a multitude of questions to which I could find no answer: "What is nature, and what is man? Why am I in this world? Did I exist before, and, if so, where did I come from? What is the object of my existence, and how will it end?"

Again the Adept, reading my thoughts, answered: "Mortal man, as you know him, is an intellectual animal, living a sort of dream-life among dream-pictures which he mistakes for realities. Real man is a celestial being, a soul dwelling temporarily within a material body. Within this organism the spiritual, divine spark finds the proper soil to generate and develop the immortal man, as has been described by Saint Paul, who speaks of that spark of divine consciousness as being sown in corruption and raised in incorruption. This spiritual man is in each person his or her personal God and Redeemer. While a man is unacquainted with the processes going on in his invisible organism, he will have little power to guide and control these processes; he will resemble a plant, which is dependent for its growth on the elements which are unconsciously brought to it by the winds and the rains, or which may accidentally be found in its surroundings; it has neither the power to prevent nor to promote its own growth. But when man obtains a knowledge of the constitution of his own soul, when he becomes conscious of the processes going on in its organism and learns to guide and control them, he will be able to command his own growth. He will become free to select or to reject the psychic influences which come within his sphere, he will become his own master and attain—so to say—psychic locomotion. He will then be as much superior to a man without such knowledge and power as an animal is superior to a plant; for while an animal may go in search of its food and select or reject what it pleases, the plant is chained to its place and depends entirely on the conditions which that one place affords. The ignorant depends on the conditions prepared for him; the wise can choose his conditions himself."

"And what will be the end and object of this?" I asked.

"The end of it," was the answer, "is that the soul of man enjoys supreme bliss in realising that she herself is everything and that there is nothing beyond her. The object is that mortal man shall become immortal, and a perfect instrument for the manifestation of divine wisdom."

I heard the answer of the Master, but I could not grasp its meaning. What could that "soul" be of which he spoke as being as big as the universe, and could my soul possess any other vehicle or organism than my visible material body?

While I was meditating, the Adept stepped with me to a window where the inaccessible mountain was seen, and pointing it out to me, he said: "Behold there the door by which you entered our stronghold; concentrate your attention upon the way you came, and seek with the eye of your soul to penetrate to the other side of the mountain."

I did so, and suddenly I found myself standing at that other side, upon the place where I had lain down to rest. Before me, upon the ground, was stretched out an apparently lifeless human figure, and to my horror I recognised it as being my own bodily self. At first everything seemed a dream, but then the thought came to me that I must have died.

There was my body; and nevertheless I was myself, and saw myself such as I had always been, with all my organs and limbs and even the same clothing which the corpse before me wore. The hat of the corpse was drawn over its eyes, and I attempted to lift it; but I might just as well have tried to lift the inaccessible mountain. There was no physical strength within my arms. I realised that my present body consisted of a state of matter differing from that of the physical plane.

I thought I must have died, and a feeling of disgust came over me, thinking that I had ever inhabited that now lifeless, grossly material form; I was so glad to be free, and had no wish to re-enter it.

But an inner voice seemed to speak to me, saying that the time of my labouring in the mundane sphere had not yet ended, and that I must return. I even felt a sort of pity for that helpless body, and the sympathy caused thereby created a strong attraction. I felt myself drawn towards that body, and was about losing my consciousness when I was called away by hearing the voice of the Master. I started as one who awakes from a dream; the Adept stood by my side, and the vision was gone.

"Know now, my friend!" he said, "the

difference between your physical and your psychical or astral organism. The divine soul has many vehicles through which it may act and manifest its powers."

"But why," I asked, "are these things not recognised by academical science?"

"On account of self-conceit," answered the Adept. "The scientists, up to a very recent date, used to discard such questions as being unworthy of their consideration, and they preferred annihilation rather than confess that there was something in the wide expanse of nature which they did not already know. The theories advanced by the theologians were not more satisfactory than those of the scientists, for they believed—or professed to believe— that man was a complete being, in a finished state, with perfect freedom of will, and, as a punishment for his subsequent bad behaviour, made a prisoner upon this planet. Furthermore, they were of the opinion that, if a man were leading a pious life, or, after leading a wicked life, obtained pardon for his sins and the favour of God, he would after his death become a celestial being, be ushered into a paradise, and live there for ever in a state of never-ending enjoyment.

"It will be acknowledged now by every independent thinker, that these theories were not

D

very satisfactory to those who desired to know
the truth. But there was nothing either to
prove or to contradict such assumptions, and,
moreover, the multitude did not think ; they
paid their clergy to do their thinking for
them.

"Since the publication of 'The Secret Doctrine' the opinions of the scientists and those
of the theologians have been equally shaken to
their foundations. The old truth which was
known to the ancients, but which had been
almost entirely forgotten during our modern
age of materialism, that man is not a finished
being, incapable of any further organic development, but that his body and his mind are continually subject to transformation and change,
and that no transformation can take place where
no substance exists, because force cannot exist
without substance, has become almost univer-
sally known. It was demonstrated to the
scientists that their science extended only to
a very small portion of that mysterious being
called Man ; that they only knew his outward
appearance, his shell, but nothing of the living
power acting within that mask which is called
the physical body. It was demonstrated to
the presumptuous theologians who believed that
man's eternal welfare or damnation depended
on their blessings or curses, that justice cannot

be separated from God, and that man's salvation depends upon his own spiritual evolution. It was made logically comprehensible to the intellect that God in man will continue to live after all the lower and imperfect elements are dissolved, and that therefore a man in whom God did not exist in a state of divinity could not, after the death of his body, jump into a higher state for which he was not fit, and which he was not able to attain while alive.

"The exposition of the essential constitution of Man, known to the Indian sages, described three hundred years ago by Theophrastus Paracelsus, and again set forth more fully and clearly than ever before by H. P. Blavatsky and other theosophical writers, is calculated to humble the pride of the scientists and the vanity of the priests. When it is once more known and digested, it will prove to the learned how little they know, and it will draw the line for the legitimate activity of the clergyman as an instructor in morals. It proves that man is not already a god, as some had imagined themselves to be. It proves that he may look like an intellectual giant, and still be, spiritually considered, only a dwarf. It demonstrates that the law which governs the growth of organisms on the physical plane is not reversed when it acts upon the corresponding organisms on the

psychical plane.   It shows that out of nothing
nothing can grow ; but that wherever there is
the germ of something, even if that germ is
invisible, something may grow and develop.

"The growth of every germ and of every
being, as far as we know it, depends on certain
conditions.   These conditions may be established
either by means of the intellectual activity of the
being itself, which has the power to surround
itself by such conditions, or they may have been
established by external causes, over which the
being has no control.   A plant or an animal
cannot grow unless it receives the food and the
stimulus which it requires ; the intellect cannot
expand unless it is fed with ideas and stimulated by reason to assimilate them ; the soul
cannot become strong unless she finds in the
lower principles the nutriment required for the
acquisition of strength, and is stimulated by
the light of wisdom to select that which she
requires."

Here again the thought occurred to me, how
agreeable and profitable it would be to live in
such a Rosicrucian convent, where everything
was rendered comfortable, no disturbing elements
being admitted.   To this the Master answered :

"One element necessary for the development
of strength is resistance.   If we enter one of
the vast pine forests of the Alps, or of the

Rocky Mountains in the United States, we find ourselves surrounded by towering trees, whose main trunks have very few branches. Upwards they rise like the masts of a ship, covered with a gray bark, naked, and without foliage. Only near the tops, that reach out of the shadows which they throw upon each other, the branches appear and spread up to the highest points, which wave their heads in the sunlight. These trees are all top-heavy; their chiefly or only well-developed parts are their heads, and all the life which they extract from the ground and the air seems to mount to their tops; while the trunks, although increasing in size as the tree grows, are left undeveloped and bare of branches. Thus they may stand and grow from year to year, and reach a mature age; but some day, sooner or later, some dark clouds collect around the snowy peaks and assume a threatening aspect; the gleam of lightnings appears among the swelling masses, the sound of thunder is heard, bolts of liquid light dart from the rents in the clouds, and suddenly the storm sweeps down from the summit into the valley. Then the work of devastation begins. These top-heavy trees, having but little strength in their feet, are mowed down by the wind like so many stems of straw in a field of wheat; there they lie rank after rank, having tumbled over each other in their fall, and their corpses encumber the mountain sides. But at the edge of the timber, and outside of the main body of the forest, looking like outposts or sentinels near the lines of a battle, there are still here and there some solitary pines to whom the storm could do no harm. They have, on account of their isolated positions, been exposed to winds all their lives; they have become used to it and grown strong. They have not been protected and sheltered by their neighbours. They are not top-heavy, for their great strong branches grow out from the trunk a few feet above the soil, continuing up to the tops, and their roots have grown through the crevices of the rocks, holding on to them with an iron grasp. They have met with resistance since the time of their youth, and, by resisting, have gained their strength.

"Thus intellectual man, growing up protected by fashion and friends in a school, college, university, or perhaps within the walls of the convent, finds himself isolated from contrary influences and meets with but little resistance. Crowded together with those who think like him, he lives and thinks like the others. Over their heads waves the banner of some accepted authority, and upon that banner are inscribed certain dogmas in which they believe without ever daring to doubt their veracity. There they grow, throwing upon each other the shadow of their ignorance, and each prevents the others from seeing the sunlight of truth. There they cram their brains with authorised opinions, learning details of our illusory life which they mistake for the real existence; they become top-heavy, for all the energy which they receive from the universal fountain of life goes to supply the brain; the soul is left without supply; the strength of character, of which the heart is the seat, suffers; the intellect is overfed and the spirit is starved. Thus they may grow up and become proud of their knowledge; but perhaps some day new and strange ideas appear on the mental horizon, a wind begins to blow, and down tumbles the banner upon which their dogmas have been inscribed, and their pride tumbles down with it.

"But not only on the physical and the intellectual plane; in the realm of the emotions, too, the same law prevails. He who desires to develop strength must not be afraid of resistance; he must obtain strength in his feet. He must be prepared to meet the wind of the lower emotions, and not be overthrown when the storms of passion arise. He should force himself to remain in contact with that which is not according to his taste, and even to harmonise

with that which appears inimical, for it is really
his friend, because it can supply him with
strength. He should learn to bear calumny
and animosity, envy and opposition; he should
learn to endure suffering, and to estimate life
at its true value. The contrary influences to
which he has been exposed may cause a tempest
to rage through his heart; but when he has
gained the power to command the tempest to
cease and to say to the excited waves: be still!
then will the first gleam of the rising sun appear
in his heart, and before its warm glow the cold
moonlight thrown out by the calculating and
reflecting brain will grow pale; a new and still
larger world than the external one will appear
before his interior vision, in which he will be
contented to live, and where he will find an
inexhaustible source of happiness, unknown to
those who live a life of the senses. Henceforth
he will require no more to speculate reflectively
about the truth, for he will see it clear in his
own heart. Henceforth he will not be required
to be exposed to storms, but may seek shelter
in a tranquil place; not because he is afraid of
the storms, which can do him no harm, but
because he wants to employ his energies for
the full development of the newly awakened
spiritual germ, instead of wasting them uselessly
on the outward plane.

"What the disciple ought to seek is to strengthen his character, which constitutes his real individuality; keeping it always in harmony with the law of divine wisdom and love. A man without strength of character is without true individuality, without self-reliance, moved only by the emotions which arise in his mind and which belong to powers foreign to his divine nature.

"Only after the attainment of a certain state of maturity, life in a solitude, isolated from contrary influences, becomes desirable and useful, and those who retire from the world as long as they need the world are attempting to ascend to the kingdom of heaven by beginning at the top of the ladder. Let him who needs the world remain in the world. The greater the temptations are by which he is surrounded, the greater will be his strength if he successfully resists. Only he who can control his mind and within his own mental sphere create the conditions which his spirit requires, is independent of all external conditions and free. He who cannot evolve a world within his own soul needs the external world to evolve his soul.

"*Unspiritual* men, therefore, who retire from the world because they are afraid of the world, cannot be considered to be heroes who

have renounced the world ; they deserve rather
to be regarded as cowards who have deserted
their ranks at the beginning of the battle
with life. Such people sometimes retire into
convents for the purpose of having a comfortable life, and in addition to that a ticket to
heaven. They imagine they do a service to
God by leading a harmless and useless life ;
for which imaginary service they expect to
obtain a reward at the end of life. But the
reward which they will receive will also exist
merely in their imagination. As the sensualist
wastes his time in the prosecution of useless
pleasures, so the bigot wastes his time in
useless ceremonies and prayers. The actions
of the former are instigated by a desire for
sensual pleasure in this life, those of the latter
by the hope for pleasure in another life ; both
are acting for the purpose of gratifying their
own selfish desires. I am unable to see any
essential difference between the motives and
morals of the two.

"But with *spiritually developed* man the
case is entirely different. The divine spark
in man exists independent of the conditions
of relative space and time ; it is eternal and
self-existent. It cannot be angered by opposition, nor irritated by contradiction, nor
be thrown into confusion by sophistry. If it

has once become conscious of its own power, it will not require the stimulus needed by the physical organism and afforded by the impressions which come through the avenues of the senses from the outer world; for it is itself that stimulus which creates worlds within its own substance. It is the Lord over all the animal elemental forces in the astral body of man, and their turmoil can neither educate nor degrade it, for it is Divinity itself in its pure state, being eternal, unchangeable, and free."

"Do you mean to say," I asked, " that all asceticism and self-denial is useless?" And the Master answered:

"It all depends upon the motive. All that the egotist does for his own selfish progress and aggrandisement is useless; it is done for an illusion, and increases his self-conceit. But this you will understand only when the consciousness of the divine state awakens within you, and you begin to realise the difference between your true and your illusive self.

"He in whom this divine principle has once awakened, he who has once practically experienced the inner life, who has visited the kingdom of heaven within his own soul, he who stands firm upon his feet, will no more need the educating influences of the contending storms of the outer world, to gain strength by resistance; nor will he experience any desire to return to the pleasures and tomfooleries of the world. He renounced nothing when he retired into the solitude; for it cannot be looked upon as an act of renunciation if we throw away a thing which is a burden to us. He cannot be called an *ascetic;* for he does not undergo any discipline or process of hardening; it is no act of self-denial to refuse things which we do not want. The true ascetic is he who lives in the world, surrounded by its temptations; he in whose soul the animal elements are still active, craving for the gratification of their desires and possessing the means for their gratification, but who by the superior power of his will conquers his animal self. Having attained that state, he may retire from the world and employ his energies for the employment and the further expansion of the spiritual power which he possesses. He will be perfectly happy, because that which he desires he can create in his own interior world. He expects no future reward in heaven; for what could heaven offer to him except happiness which he already possesses. He desires no other good but to create good for the world.

"If you could establish theosophical academies where intellectual and spiritual development would go hand in hand, where a new science could be taught, based upon a true knowledge of the fundamental laws of the universe, and where at the same time man would be taught how to obtain mastery over himself, you would confer the greatest possible benefit upon the world. Such a convent would, moreover, afford immense advantages for the advancement of intellectual research. The establishment of a number of such places of learning would dot the mental horizon of the world with stars of the first magnitude, from which rays of intellectual light would stream and penetrate the world. Standing upon a far higher plane than the material science of our times, a new and far greater field would be laid open for investigation and research in these centres. Knowing all the different opinions of the highest accepted authorities, and not being bound by an orthodox scientific creed, having at their service all the results of the investigations of the learned, but not being bound to their systems by a belief in their infallibility, such people would be at liberty to think freely. Their convents would become centres of intelligence, illuminating the world ; and if their power of self-control would grow in equal proportion with the development of their intellect, they would soon be able to enter adeptship."

The Adept had spoken these words with unusual warmth, as if he intended to appeal to my sympathy and to induce me to use my efforts to establish such convents; there was a look of pity in his eyes, as if he exceedingly regretted the state of poor ignorant humanity, with whose Karma he was not permitted to interfere forcibly, according to the established rules of his order. I, too, regretted my own inability to establish such academies, and for once I wished that I were rich, so as to be able to make at least an attempt with one such establishment. But immediately the Imperator saw my thought in my mind, and said:

"You mistake; it is not the want of money which prevents us from executing this idea; it is the impossibility of finding at present the proper kind of people to inhabit the convent after it is established. Indeed, we would be poor alchemists if we could not produce gold in any desirable quantity, if some real benefit for humanity could be effected thereby, and of this I shall convince you, if you desire it. But gold is a curse to mankind, and we do not wish to increase the curse from which humanity suffers. Distribute gold among men, and you will only create a craving for more; give them power, and you will transform them into devils. No; it is not gold that we need; it is men who thirst after true wisdom. There are thousands who desire knowledge, but few who desire wisdom. Intellectual development, sagacity, craftiness, cunning, are to-day mistaken for spiritual development, but this conception is wrong; animal cunning is not intelligence, craftiness is not wisdom, and most of your learned men are the last ones who can bear the truth. Even many of your would-be occultists and so-called Rosicrucians have taken up their investigations merely for the purpose of gratifying their idle curiosity, while others desire to pry into the secrets of nature to obtain knowledge which they hope to employ for the attainment of selfish ends. Give us men or women who desire nothing else but the truth, and we will take care of their needs. How much money will it require to lodge a person who cares nothing for comfort? What will it take to furnish the kitchen for those who have no desire for dainties? What libraries will be required for those who can read in the book of nature? What external pictures will please those who wish to avoid a life of the senses and to retire within their own selves? What terrestrial scenery shall be selected for those who live within the paradise of their souls? What company will please those who converse with their own higher self? How can we amuse those who live in the presence of God?"

Here the Adept paused for a moment, and then continued, saying: "Verily the theosophical monastery of which I dream is even superior to ours. It is located far away from this earth, and yet it can be reached without trouble and without expense. Its monks and nuns have risen above the sphere of self. They have a temple of infinite dimensions, pervaded by the spirit of sanctity, which is the common possession of all. There the differentiation of the Universal Soul ceases, and Unification takes place. It is a convent where there exists no difference of sex, of taste, opinion, and desire; where vice cannot enter; where none are born, or marry, or die, but where they live like the angels; each one constituting the centre of a power for good; each one immersed in an infinite ocean of light; each one able to see all he desires to see, to know all he wants to know, growing in strength and expanding in size, until he embraces the All and is one with it."

For a moment it seemed as if the soul of the Adept had gone and visited that blissful state of Nirvana, a state of which we mortals cannot conceive; but soon the light returned into his eyes, and he smilingly excused himself, saying that he had permitted himself to be carried away by the sublimity of this idea. I ventured to say that probably millions of ages would pass away before mankind would arrive at that state.

" Alas !" he answered, " the conditions which our present state of civilisation imposes upon its followers are now such as to force the vast majority of humanity to employ nearly all their time and energy in an outward direction, instead of employing them for their inward growth. Each man has a certain amount of energy which he may call his own. If he wastes his energy on the outward plane, either for the attainment of sensual gratification or in intellectual pursuits, he will have nothing left to nourish the divine germ in his heart. If he continually concentrates his mind outwardly, there will be no inward concentration of thought, which is absolutely necessary for the attainment of self-knowledge. The labouring classes, men of commerce, scientists, doctors, lawyers, and clergymen are all actively engaged in outward affairs, and find little time for the inward con- centration of their powers. The majority are continually occupied in running after shadows and illusions, which are at best only useful as long as they last, but whose usefulness ceases when the heart ceases to beat. Their time and energy are taken up in procuring what they call

E

the ' necessaries of life,' and they excuse themselves by saying that it is their misfortune to
be so situated as to be forced to procure them.
Nature, however, cares nothing for our excuses ;
the law of cause and effect is blind and inaccessible to argumentation.   A man climbing
over a mountain top and falling over a precipice,
is as much in danger of breaking his neck as if
he had jumped down voluntarily ; a man who is
not able to progress will be left as far behind
as one who does not desire to progress.   But
nature is not so cruel as she appears to be to the
superficial observer.   That which man requires
for the purpose of living is very little indeed,
and can usually be easily obtained ; for nature
has amply provided for all of her children, and
if they cannot all obtain their proper share
then there must be something seriously wrong,
either with them individually or with the social
organisation as a whole.   There is undoubtedly
a great deal wrong in our social organisation,
and our philosophers and politicians are continually trying to remedy it.   They will succeed
in their task when they succeed in making the
laws of the human world harmonise with the
laws of nature, and not before.   That event
may take place in the far distant future.   We
have not the time to wait for it.   Let each one
attempt to restore harmony in his own in-

dividual organism and live according to natural laws, and the harmony of the social organism as a whole will be restored."

The words of the Adept caused me some irritation, for I loved the comforts of life. A spirit of contradiction arose within me and caused me to say : " Would you, then, do away with all luxuries, which at our present stage of civilisation have become necessities ? Would you have us return to the semi-animal state of our forefathers, living as savages in the woods ? I know there are certain cranks that harbour such views."

" Not so," answered the Adept. " The great bulk of those things which are said to be the necessities of life are only artificially created necessities, and millions of people lived and attained old age long before many of the things which our modern civilisation considers as absolutely necessary had been discovered or invented. The term ' necessity ' has a relative meaning ; and to a king a dozen of palaces, to a nobleman a carriage and four, may appear as much a necessity as to a beggar a bottle of whisky, or to a fashionable man a new swallow-tail coat. To get rid at once of all such fancied necessities and the trouble which is imposed upon us to attain them, the shortest and surest way is to rise above such necessities and to consider them not to be necessary at all. Then a great amount of our energy would become free, and might be employed for the acquisition of that which is really necessary, because it is eternal and permanent, while that which serves merely temporal purposes ends in time.

"There are thousands of people engaged in prying into the details of the constitution of external objects and in learning the chemical and physiological processes going on therein, and some are sacrificing their soul and extinguishing the spark of divinity within themselves by perpetrating the most inhuman cruelties upon their fellow-beings for the purpose of gratifying their scientific curiosity and making useless discoveries for the promotion of their ambition; but they do not manifest the least desire to know their own real self, although it would seem that such a knowledge is far more important. Modern science says that she wants to know the laws of nature in all their minute ramifications, and yet she pays no attention whatever to the universal and fundamental law from which all these ramifications spring; and thus she resembles an insect crawling over a fallen leaf and imagining thereby to learn the qualities of the tree. It is surely the prerogative of intellectual man to investigate intellectually all the departments of nature ; but the investigation of external things is only of secondary importance to the attainment of knowledge of our own interior powers. All primary powers act from within ; effects are secondary to causes. He who considers the knowledge of external things to be more important than the knowledge of God, possesses very little wisdom indeed."

"God !" I exclaimed. " What can we know about God ? How can you prove that such a being exists ? "

To this answered the Adept : " I am sorry for a man who is so far backward in his course of spiritual evolution that he is not yet able to recognise the presence of God in everything. The supreme spirit which pervades, embraces, and penetrates everything, being the very essence, soul, and life of all things in the universe, from the atom up to the whole solar system, is beyond all mental conception. If He could be grasped by the human intellect, that intellect would have to be greater than God. There is nothing real but God. Nature itself is only a manifestation of His power. Let no man expect that somebody will prove to him the existence of God ; but let every one seek to be himself a living witness of His presence and power by becoming god-like and divine by His divine grace. Man is destined

to restore within himself the divine image.
When he realises the divine ideal within his
heart, his pilgrimage through manifold incarnations will have ended and the object of his
existence be accomplished.   Peace be with
you ! "

As the Adept finished this sentence, a sound
as if produced by the tinkling of small silver
bells was heard in the air above our heads.
I looked up, but nothing was to be seen from
which that sound could have proceeded.

" This is the signal," said the Adept, " that
the members of our order are assembled in
the Refectory.   Let us go to join their company.
Some refreshment will undoubtedly be welcome
to you."

IV

THE REFECTORY

WE stepped out into the corridor and entered the garden. The palm trees and exotic plants, by which we were surrounded, formed a strong contrast to the weird and desolate scenery, with its fields of ice and scrub-pines, which I had seen before entering this enchanted valley. High bushes of fuchsias alternated with rose-bushes, and all were covered with the most beautiful flowers; the air was perfumed with the odour of many varieties of hyacinths, heliotropes, and other plants whose names I do not remember. Nevertheless the place was not a hot-house, for there was no other roof over it than the clear blue sky. I wondered whether perhaps the garden was heated from below the surface, and the thought came into my mind that so much luxury seemed not to agree with the view, expressed by the Adept, that those who live within the paradise of their own souls do not care for external sensual gratification. But again the

Imperator seemed to know my thought even before it had taken a definite form in my mind, and said :

" We have created these illusions to make your visit to this place an agreeable one in every respect. All these trees and plants which you see require no gardener, and are inexpensive ; they cost us nothing but an effort of our imagination."

I went up to one of the rose-bushes and broke one of the roses. It was a real rose, as real as I had ever seen before; its odour was sweet, and it had just unfolded its leaves in the rays of the midday sun.

"Surely," I said, "this rose which I hold in my hand cannot be an illusion, or an effect of my imagination ? "

" No," answered the Adept, " it is not produced by your own imagination, but it is a product of the imagination of nature, whose processes can be guided by the spiritual will of the Adept. The whole world, with its solid planets, its mountains of granite, its oceans and rivers, the whole earth with all its multifarious forms, is nothing else but a product of the imagination of the *Universal Mind*, which is the *creator* of forms. Forms are nothing real, they are merely illusions or shapes of substance; a form without substance is unthinkable and cannot exist. But the only substance of which we know is the universal primordial element of matter, constituting the substance of Universal Mind, the *A'kâsa*. This element of matter is invisibly present everywhere; but only when it assumes a certain state of density, sufficient to resist the penetrating influence of the terrestrial light, does it come within the reach of your sensual perception, and assume for you an objective shape. The universal power of will penetrates all things. Guided by the spiritual intelligence of the Adept, whose consciousness pervades all his surroundings, it creates in the Universal Mind those shapes which the Adept imagines; for the sphere of the Universal Mind is his own. By an occult process, which cannot be at present explained to you, but which exists principally in a motion of will, the shapes thus created in the mind-substance of the Adept are rendered dense, and thereby become objective and visible to you."

"I acknowledge," I said, "that this is still incomprehensible to me. Can an image formed in your head come out of your head and assume a material form?"

The Adept seemed to be amused at my ignorance, and smilingly answered: "Do you believe that the sphere of mind in which man

lives exists only within the circumference of
his skull? I should be sorry for such a man;
for he would not be able to see or experience
anything whatever beyond the processes going
on in that part of his mind contained within
his skull. The whole world would be to him
nothing but impenetrable and incomprehensible
darkness. He would not be able to see the
sun or any external object; for man can perceive nothing except that which exists within
his own mind. Fortunately for man, the sphere
of the mind of each individual man reaches as
far as the stars. It reaches as far as his power
of perception reaches. His mind comes in contact with all things, however distant they may
be from his physical body. Thus his mind—
not his brain—receives the impressions, and
these impressions come to his consciousness
within his physical brain, which is merely the
centre in which the messages of the mind are
received."

After giving this explanation, the Adept,
evidently still seeing some doubts in my mind,
directed me to look at a magnolia tree which
stood at a short distance. It was a tree of
perhaps sixty feet in height, and covered with
great, white, beautiful flowers. While I looked,
the tree began to appear less and less dense.
The green foliage faded into gray, so that the

white blossoms could hardly be distinguished from the leaves; it became more and more shadowy and transparent; it seemed to be merely the ghost of a tree, and finally it disappeared entirely from view.

"Thus," continued the Adept, "you see that tree stood in the sphere of my mind as it stood in yours. We are all living within the sphere of each other's mind, and he in whom the power of spiritual perception has been developed may at all times see the images created in the mind of another. The Adept creates his own images; the ordinary mortal lives in the products of the imagination of others, either in those of the imagination of nature, or in those which have been created by other minds. We live in the paradise of our own consciousness, and the objects which you behold exist in the realm of our consciousness; but these spheres are not narrow. They may be expanded far beyond the limits of the visible objects around us, and continue to expand until they become one with the whole Universe.

"The power of the imagination is yet too little known to mankind, else they would better beware of what they think. If a man thinks ﬁ good or an evil thought, that thought calls into existence a corresponding form or power within the sphere of his mind, which may assume density and become living, and continue to live long after the physical body of the man who created it has died. It will accompany his soul after death, because the creations are attracted to their creator."

"Does, then," I asked, "every evil thought, or the imagination of something evil, create that evil and cause it to exist as a living entity?"

"Not so," answered the Imperator. "Every thought calls into existence the form or power of which we think; but these things have no life until life is infused into them by the Will. If they do not receive life from the Will, they are like shadows and soon fade away. If this were not the case, men could never read of a crime without mentally committing it, and thereby creating most vicious Elementals. You may imagine evil deeds of all kinds; but, unless you have a desire to perform them, the creations of your imagination obtain no life. But if you desire to perform them, if your will is so evil that you would be willing to perform them if you had the external means to do so, then it may perhaps be as bad for you as if you had actually committed them, and you create thereby a living although invisible power of evil. It is the Will which endows the creations of imagination with life, because *Will* and *Life* are fundamentally identical."

Seeing a doubt arise in my mind, he continued : " If I speak of the Will as a life-giving power, I am speaking of the spiritual will-power which resides in the heart. A will-power merely exercised by the brain is like the cold light of the moon, which has no power to warm the forms upon which it falls. The life-giving will-power comes from the heart, and acts like the rays of the sun which call life into action in minerals, plants, and animals. It is that which man desires with his heart, not that which he merely imagines with his brain, which has real power. Fortunately for mankind in general, this spiritual power which calls the creations of the imagination into objective visible existence is in the possession of very few, else the world would be filled with living materialised monsters, which would devour mankind ; for there are in our present state of civilisation more people who harbour evil desires than such as desire the good. But their will is not spiritual enough to be powerful ; it comes more from the brain than from the heart ; it is usually only strong enough to harm him who created the evil thought, and to leave others unaffected. Thus you see how important it is that men should not come into possession of spiritual powers until they become virtuous and good. These are mysteries which in former times were kept very secret, and which ought not to be revealed to the vulgar."

We entered through a Gothic portal into a hall. The light fell through four high windows into the room, which was of an octagonal form. In the midst of this room stood a round table surrounded by chairs, and the corners formed by the sides of the octagon were provided with furniture of various kinds. There were quite a number of the Brothers assembled, some of whom I recognised from having seen their pictures in historical representations; but what astonished me above all was that there were two ladies present—one appearing very tall and dignified, the other one of smaller stature and of a more delicate, but not less noble, appearance, and exceedingly beautiful. To find *ladies* in the monastery of the Brothers of the Golden and Rosy Cross was a fact which surprised and staggered me, and my confusion was evidently observed by all present; but after I had been introduced to all the persons present—or, to express it more correctly, after they had all been introduced to me, for they all seemed to know me and not to need my introduction—the tall lady took my hand and led me to the table, while she smilingly spoke the following words :

" Why should you be so surprised, my friend, to see Adepts inhabiting female forms in company of those whose forms appear to be of a male character ? What has intelligence to do with the sex of the body ? Where the sexual instincts end, there ends the influence of sex. Come, now, and take this chair by my side, and have some of this delicious fruit."

The table was covered with a variety of excellent fruits, some of which I had never seen before, and which do not grow in this country. The illustrious company took their seats, and a conversation ensued in which all took part. I only too deeply felt my own inferiority while in this place, but every one seemed to exert his powers to reassure me and to make me imagine that I was their equal. The Brothers and Sisters hardly tasted the food, but they seemed to be pleased to see me enjoy it, and in fact my morning walk and the pure air of the mountain had given me a very good appetite. The noble lady next to whom I was seated soon succeeded in making my embarrassment vanish, answered my questions in regard to the causes of certain occult phenomena, and made a few practical experiments to illustrate her doctrines. The following may serve as an example of the powers she possessed to create illusions.

We came to speak of the intrepidity and undaunted courage which he must possess who desires to enter the realm of occult research : "For," she said, "the whole elemental world, with all its monstrosities and animal elements, is opposed to man's spiritual progress. The animals (Elementals) in the animal principle of man's constitution live on his life and on the substance of his animal elements. If the divine spirit awakens within the heart of man and sends its light into those animal elements, the substance on which these parasites live becomes destroyed, and they begin to rage like other famished beasts. They fight for their lives and for their food, and they are therefore the greatest impediments and opponents to the spiritual progress of man. They live in the lower regions of the soul of man, and are, under normal conditions, invisible to the external senses, although under certain conditions they may even become visible and objective. They live in families, and reproduce their species like our terrestrial animals ; they fight with each other and eat each other up. If a man's selfish desires, such as are of a minor type, are all swallowed up by some great master-passion, it merely shows that a *monster elemental* has grown in his soul and devoured all the minor elementals."

I answered that it was impossible for me to believe that man was such a living and walking menagerie, and said I wished I could see one of these elementals, so as to realise what it was.

"Would you not be afraid," she asked, "if such a vicious thing were to appear?"

I began to boast of my bravery, and said that I was never afraid of anything which I could see with my eyes and reach with my hands; that fear was the outcome of ignorance, and that knowledge dispelled all fear.

"You are right," she answered; "but will you be so kind as to hand me that basket with pears."

I stretched forth my hand after the basket with pears, which stood in the midst of the table, and as I was about to grasp it, a horrible rattlesnake rose up between the fruit; rearing its head and making a noise with its rattles as if in great anger. Horror-struck, I withdrew my hand, barely escaping its venomous bite; but while I stared at it, the serpent coiled itself up again among the pears, its glistening scales disappeared in the basket, and it was gone.

F

"If you had dared to grasp the snake," said one of the Brothers, who had witnessed the scene, "you would have found it to be merely a shadow."

"The Will," remarked the Imperator, "is not merely a life-giving power; it is also a destroyer. It causes the atoms of primordial matter to collect around a centre; it holds them together, or it may disperse them again into space. It is Brahma, Vishnu, and Siva in one; the creator, maintainer, and destroyer of form."

"These Elementals," said the beautiful lady, "master us if we do not master them. If we attack them without fear, they can do us no harm; our thought is destructive to them; because they are the creations of our own thoughts."

The conversation during our breakfast turned to occultism and kindred subjects. "Occultism and alchemy," said one of the Brothers, "are at once the most difficult and the easiest things to grasp. They are indeed easy to comprehend, if we only look at the mysteries of nature by the light of wisdom, with which each human being, except an idiot, has been endowed by nature at the time of his birth. But if in the place of the sun of divine wisdom, the artificial candlelight of false logic, sophistry, and speculation has been lit by irrational education, man steps out of his natural state and becomes unnatural. The images of the eternal truths—which were mirrored in his mind while he was a child and innocent, and not sufficiently intellectually developed to understand them—become, by the time that his intellect is developed, so distorted and perverted by prejudices and misconceptions that their original forms are no more recognisable, and, instead of seeing the real, man only sees the hallucinations which his fancy has created."

"Do you mean to say," I asked, "that man can possibly know anything about the nature of things, besides that which has been taught to him by his books?"

"Does the child," asked the Adept, in answer to my question, "need an instructor to explain to it the use of its mother's breasts? Do the cattle require books on botany to know which herbs are poisonous and which are wholesome? Those artificial systems which have been created by man, and which are therefore unnatural, cannot be found in the book of nature; to know the name of a thing which has been invented for it by man, the child needs man's instructions; but the essential attributes of a thing are independent of the name given to it.

Shakespeare says that a rose would have an agreeable odour, even if it were called by some other name. At the present stage of education, natural philosophers know all about the artificial names and classifications of things, but very little about their interior qualities. What does a modern botanist know about the *signatures* of plants, by which the Occultist recognises the medicinal and occult properties of plants as soon as he sees them? The animals have remained natural, while man became unnatural. The sheep does not need to be instructed by a zoölogist to seek to escape if a tiger approaches; it knows by his signature, and without argumentation, that he is his enemy. Is it not much more important for the sheep to know the ferocious character of the tiger, than to be informed that the latter belongs to genus *Felis?* If by some miracle a sheep should become intellectual, it might learn so much about the external form, anatomy, physiology, and genealogy of the tiger, that it would lose sight of its internal character and be devoured by it. Absurd as this example may appear, it is nevertheless the true representation of what is done in your schools every day. There the rising generation receive what they call a scientific education. They are taught all about the external form of man, and how that form may be comfortably fed, lodged, and housed, but the sight of the real man who occupies that form is entirely lost, his needs are neglected, he is starved, ill-treated, and crucified, and some of your 'great lights of science' have become so short-sighted that they even deny that he is."

"But," I objected, "is it not a great prerogative which intellectual man enjoys over the animal creation, that he possesses an intellect by which he is able to understand the attributes of things which the animal merely instinctively feels ?"

"True," said the Brother ; "but man should use his intellect in accordance with reason, and not oppose his intellect to the same. Instinct in animals is the activity in the animal organism of that principle whose action in human beings is called reason. It is the faculty of the soul to feel the truth ; while the function of the intellect is to understand that which is instinctively or intuitively felt by the soul, or perceived by the exterior senses. If the intellect were to act only in harmony with reason, all intellectual human beings would not only be intellectual, but would also be wise ; but we know from our daily experience that intellectuality is not necessarily accompanied by wisdom, that often those who are most cunning are also most vicious, and the most learned often the most unreasonable."

"The first and most important step," continued the Brother, "which man must take, if he desires to obtain spiritual power, is to become natural. Only when he has thrown off all his unnatural qualities can he hope to become spiritually strong. If he were to become spiritual before he becomes natural, he would be an unnatural spiritual monster. Such monsters have existed and still exist. They are the spiritual powers of evil acting through human forms; they are the Adepts of Black Magic, sorcerers and villains of various grades."

"Then," I said, "I presume that great criminals are to a certain extent black magicians."

"Not necessarily so," answered the Brother. "The majority of evil-doers do evil, not for the love of evil, but for the purpose of attaining some selfish purpose. The villains who are on the road to Black Magic do evil because they love it, in the same sense as those who are on the road to true adeptship perform good merely because they love good. But whether man performs good or evil acts, a constant or frequent repetition of such acts causes him finally to perform them instinctively, and thus his own nature becomes gradually either identified with

good or with evil. He who merely tortures a
fly for the sake of torturing it, and because he
is pleased to do so, is farther progressed on the
road to villainy and absolute evil with conse-
quent destruction, than he who murders a man
because he imagines it to be necessary for his
own protection that he should murder him."

Here the conversation began to turn about
White Magic and the wonderful powers of certain Tibetan Adepts. The Imperator, who had
recently visited them, gave a detailed account
of his visit. But, strange as it may appear,
while all the details of the other part of our
conversation remained deeply engraven in my
memory, the account given by the Imperator
about that visit is entirely effaced from my recollection, and I cannot remember anything
whatever about it. It is as if its recollection had been purposely eradicated from my
mind.

After our breakfast was over, the Imperator
recommended me to the care of the two Lady-
Adepts, and told me that he would soon rejoin
us to show me his alchemical laboratory. I
then accompanied my two protectors into the
beautiful garden.

V

RECOLLECTIONS OF PAST LIVES

WE passed through an alley formed by oleander bushes in full bloom, and arrived at a small round pavilion standing upon a little eminence, which afforded a beautiful view of the country and the tall mountain tops in the distance. The roof of the pavilion was supported by marble columns surrounded by ivy, which grew around the pillars and nearly covered the roof, hanging down at intervals in the open spaces. We seated ourselves, and after a short pause, my friend, whom I will call Leila, said: "I owe you an explanation in regard to the remarks I made when I saw your astonishment at seeing the female sex represented among the Brothers of the Golden and Rosy Cross. Your intuition told you right. It does not indeed very often happen that an individual attains adeptship while inhabiting a female organism, because such an organism is not as well adapted as a male one to develop energy and strength, and it is, therefore frequently the case that those women who have far advanced on the road to adeptship must reincarnate in a male organism, before they can achieve the final result. Nevertheless, exceptions are found. You know that the organism of a man is not fundamentally different from that of a woman, and in each human being are male and female elements combined. In women usually the female elements preponderate, and in men the male ones are usually most active, although we meet with women of a masculine character, and with men who are of a womanish nature. In a perfect human being the male and female elements are nearly equally strong, with a slight preponderance of the male element, which represents the productive power in nature, while the female element represents the formative principle. This occult law, which to explain at present would lead us deep into the mysteries of nature, will become comprehensible to you if you will study the laws of harmony. You will then find that the *Moll*-accord is the harmonious counterpart of the *Dur*-accord, but that the greatest beauty finds its expression in *Dur*. Other and numerous analogies may be found, and we shall leave it to your own ingenuity to find them out.

" If you therefore find an Adept inhabiting a female organism, you will be right in concluding that such an abnormal circumstance is due to some extraordinary conditions and experiences

through which such an Adept has passed during
his last incarnation.   A plant in a hot-house will
grow faster than one which is not cared for, and,
likewise, extraordinary suffering may cause the
early development of the flower of spirituality,
which without such suffering would have taken
place, perhaps, much later in some other incarnation."

This revelation stirred my curiosity, and I
begged the lady to give me an account of her
past life, as it was before she became an
Adept.

"It is sometimes painful," answered Leila,
"to dwell on the memories of the past, but
perhaps our sister Helen will give you such an
account of her life."

The lady addressed smiled, and said : "I will
certainly do so to afford a pleasure to our
visitor, but my life in comparison with yours
has been very uninteresting.   If you will proceed
with your history, I will add mine at the end."

"Very well, then," answered Leila ; "but to
simplify matters, and to save time, I will show
you its pictorial representation in the Astral
Light.   Look upon the table before you."

I looked upon the polished surface of the
round marble table standing in the centre of
the pavilion, and, as I looked, there appeared
upon its surface the life-like image of a battle-

field. There were the contending armies fight-
ing with swords and spears, men on horseback
and men on foot, knights in glistening armour,
and common soldiers. Hot grows the fight;
the dead and wounded cover the ground, and
the soldiers to the left begin to give way, while
those to the right press forward. Suddenly
there appears at the left a beautiful woman,
dressed in armour, carrying a sword in one
hand and in the other a banner. Her features
resemble those of the Lady-Adept. At sight
of her the men to the left seem to become filled
with strength, while their enemies seem to be
stricken with terror. The latter flee, pursued
by the men on the left, and a shout of triumph
arises, and the picture fades away.

Now there appears another picture upon the
table. It seems to be the interior of a Catholic
church. There is a great assembly of digni-
taries of church and state, of knights and
nobles, bishops and priests, and a multitude
of people. In front of the altar kneels an
armoured knight, who seems to be the king, and
a bishop, ornamented with the insignia of his
office, puts a golden crown upon his head; but
by the side of the king stands again that noble-
looking woman, with a smile of triumph upon
her face and holding a banner. A solemn
music is heard, but as the crown rests upon the

head of the king and he arises, a thousand
voices hail him, and the picture fades away.

The next picture represents a dungeon filled
with instruments of torture, such as were used
at the time of the Inquisition.   There are some
men dressed in black, and in their eyes burns
the fire of hate ; there are others dressed in
red ; they are evidently the executioners.   Some
people with torches appear, and in their midst
is Leila bound with chains.   She looks at the
men in black with pity and contempt.   They
ask her some silly questions, which she re-
fuses to answer, and then they begin to
torture her in a most cruel manner.   I averted
my sight, and when I looked again, the picture
was gone.

In its place appeared another.   There is a
pile of wood, and in its midst a stake to which
a chain is fastened.   A procession approaches,
led by villainous-looking monks and guarded by
soldiers.   Crowds of people surround the pile,
but they give way as the procession approaches.
In the midst of the monks and hangmen walks
Leila, looking pale and emaciated from torture
and sufferings ; her hands are tied, and a rope
is fastened round her neck.   She mounts the
pile and is fastened to the stake.   She attempts
to speak, but the praying monks dash water
into her face to force her to remain silent.   A

hangman appears with a brand of fire; the wood begins to burn; the flames touch the body of the beautiful woman. I desired to see no more; I buried my face in my hands; I knew who Leila was.

After I had recovered from the impression which this horrible sight had made upon my mind, I expressed to Leila my admiration for her valour and virtue. I had always admired her as a historical character, and desired to see her portrait. Now she stood before me, the living original, youthful and strong, noble and beautiful, and yet, according to history, over 450 years of age.

It is useless to attempt to conceal a thought in the presence of the Adepts. Leila observed my thought, and answered it.

"No," she said, "I am much older than you think. I and you, and we all, are as old as creation. When the spirit began to breathe after the Great *Pralaya* was over, sending out of the centre the light of the *Logos*, which called the world into existence, we lived already, and we shall continue to live until this light returns to its source. God in us knows no age; He is eternal and independent of the conditions of time. Nor can our spiritual bodies be destroyed by fire."

"But," I said, "your body was destroyed by fire."

"That which was destroyed," answered Leila, "was merely the grossest material substance of my physical organisation. As the fire consumed the gross matter, my ethereal form arose above the fire and the smoke; it was invisible to the multitude present, whose senses are so gross that they can only perceive gross matter; but it was visible to the Adepts who were present in their ethereal forms, and who took care of me, and after a short period of unconsciousness I awoke again to external life. Gradually my body hardened again by the action of the influences prevailing in my new home, and therefore I am now as visible and tangible to you as if I were still inhabiting my material form."

"Then, I presume," I said, "that the astral body of every human being or animal could be so hardened, after having left the physical form, and thus the spirits of the dead could be made to appear in a tangible and visible form."

"It could be done, and it has often been done," answered Leila, "by the vile practices of the necromantic art. It can be done with the earth-bound astral shades of some who have suddenly died by accident or murder, and in whose astral forms is therefore still a great deal of molecular adhesion; but the astral forms of those who have died long ago cannot be thus evoked, because their astral corpses have already been decomposed by the influences of the astral plane. But those 'materialised' forms have no life of their own, and cannot endure. They only live by the life-principle infused into them by the necromancer who performs such acts consciously, or by the *medium* who performs them unconsciously. To enable an astral form to continue to live after the death of the physical form, it must have attained spiritual life during the life of the physical body."

"Surely," I said, "in every human being the astral form contained within the physical body has life."

"True," she answered, "but not in every human being is it the centre of life and of consciousness. In ordinary mortals the seat of life is in the blood contained in the veins and arteries of the physical form, and the astral form lives only, so to say, from the reflex of that physical life. In the Adept, the centre of life and consciousness has been established in the organism of his soul, clothed with the astral form, and is therefore self-conscious and independent of the life of the

physical body. I had already during former
incarnations acquired that life and consciousness
of the spirit. I was on the way to adeptship
before I was born in a peasant's hut. During
my childhood I had spiritual intercourse with
Adepts, although I knew them not intellectually, because my intellectual activity, the
result of my physical organisation, was then
not sufficiently perfect to understand that which
my spirit perceived. But," she continued, "let
us drop these metaphysical speculations, which
I see fatigue your brain, and which are still
more difficult of comprehension, in that there
is no rule without some exception, and the
laws of nature are liable to produce endless
varieties."

"Many thanks for your kindness in giving
me so much information," I said; "but permit
me to ask one more question. What were
the voices you heard and the apparition you
saw? Was it truly the archangel Michael
who gave you your mission and aided you in
your victories?"

"No," was the reply. "Angels do not interfere personally in mundane matters; spiritually
developed man is higher than they. It was
the influence of one of our Brothers, who
was formerly a great warrior and patriot,
whose power entered within myself and took

the shape of a knight, representing the arch-angel for whom I always had a great veneration and whose image was foremost in my mind . . . But see. . . ."

To my great astonishment Leila became suddenly transformed into the luminous shape of a knight in a brilliant armour, which shone like the sun, so that I had to avert my eyes for fear of getting blinded. The apparition disappeared within a few moments, and Leila stood there again in her previous form.

I had for a long time observed the features of the other Lady-Adept; and it seemed to me as if I had seen her somewhere, perhaps in my dreams. Yes, I remember that when I was a mere child I once had a vision, while in a state between sleeping and waking, when it seemed to me as if an angel or a super-terrestrial being, clad in white and holding a white lily in her hand, were floating in the air over my head, extending the lily towards me. How often had I prayed in my heart to see that beautiful form again; and now, if I did not mistake, this lady was the form I had seen in my dream.

She was of exceeding great beauty; her long, black, waving hair formed a strong contrast to her plain, white, and flowing robe, covering her form with graceful folds. Her

G

tint was pale and delicate, her profile was pure Greek; her dark eyes seemed to penetrate to the innermost centre of my soul, and to kindle there a fire of pure love and admiration without any admixture of the animal element.

"My life," said Helen, "was one of little importance. I was born at St. Petersburg, and my father was an officer in the imperial army. He died while I was very young, and left his family in great poverty. Besides the company of my mother, my relatives, and a teacher, there was nothing to attract me to earth. My mind unfolded and revelled in superterrestrial joys; I loved poetry; I loved to look at the clouds sailing in the sky, and to see in them objects of beauty; I communicated in spirit with the heroes of the past. But the development of my physical form could not keep step with the unfoldment of the mind. Cold, starvation, and want hastened its dissolution. After having reached my eighteenth year, I left my wasted, consumptive form, and was kindly received by the Brothers."

Her plain and modest tale filled my heart with pity. "And was there no one," I said, "among your country people intelligent enough to perceive your genius and to give you support?"

"They erected a costly monument to my

memory," she answered, "after my body had succumbed. A part of the money expended for it would have procured me the necessaries to prolong my life. Those who knew me while living admired my poetry and my talents, but they were poor like myself. But let that pass. The conditions under which men live are the effects of previously acquired Karma. My poverty and suffering were my gain. I have cause to be well satisfied with my lot."

While the lady spoke, I scanned her features. Was it really she who had appeared to me years ago in a dream? Was it she who waved that lily as if pronouncing a blessing? Was it the magnetic current which seemed to stream through that symbol into the depths of my heart, and to call there a higher life into activity? Could that event have been a dream? Did it not fill my whole being with happiness at the time when it happened? Did its memory not remain deeply engraved in my heart, when thousands of other dreams had faded away?

Helen rose, and reaching out through one of the open spaces between the pillars, she broke a white lily flower which grew close by the wall. This she gave to me, and said, "Keep this flower; it will not fade like a dream; and when you see it you will know that I am not a product of hallucination."

I thanked her and begged her to remain my protector in the future, as she had been in the past. To this she answered : " We can only assist those who protect themselves. We can only influence those who are ready to receive our influence. We can only approach those who spiritually approach our own sphere. Love causes mutual attraction ; the pure will be attracted to the pure, the evil ones to that which is evil. To give presupposes the capacity to receive on the part of him who is to receive. The sunlight is open to all, but not all are able to see it. The eternal fountain of truth is inexhaustible and universal; but those who open their hearts to the sunshine of truth are few. Seek continually to rise above the sphere of selfishness, and you will be in company of those who have thrown off their animal elements and live in the spirit."

As the lady finished speaking, another Adept approached the pavilion. He was a man of small stature, but with a highly intellectual expression upon his face which at once indicated that he must be a Master. His head was almost bald on the top, and showed a most remarkable formation of his skull ; at each side, however, there were gray locks of hair, and I immediately recognised in him one whose picture I had often seen and whose presence I had often felt, and whom I will call Theodorus. He had been a great Adept and Rosicrucian during his earthly life; he had been a great physician, and performed most wonderful cures. He had been a great alchemist, and knew the secret of the *Cross* and the *Rose*, of the *Red Lion* and the *White Eagle.*

As he entered, he announced that the Imperator had been called away to attend to some important affairs connected with politics on the mundane plane. He jocularly remarked that he had gone to prevent a certain statesman from committing an act of imbecility, which would, if he did not succeed in stopping it, be productive of a great war. He was therefore deputed by the Imperator to show me the alchemical laboratory and to correct some of my misconceptions in regard to alchemy. I was rather reluctant to leave the presence of the ladies, and I would have been willing to die at that moment to enable my soul to remain in their presence; but I could not with propriety decline the invitation. The ladies permitted me to retire, and I went with Theodorus into the halls of the Monastery.

VI

THE ALCHEMICAL LABORATORY

WE went through a beautiful and broad corridor, all along whose sides stood finely executed marble statues representing the gods and goddesses of antiquity, and busts of the heroes of olden times. "These statues," my companion remarked, "represent the elemental principles and powers of nature, and they were thus personified by the ancients to bring the attributes of these principles within the conceptive power of the mind. None of the old Greeks and Romans, except the most ignorant, ever believed that Zeus, Pluto, Neptune, &c., were existing personalities; nor did they ever worship them as such. They were merely symbols and personifications of formless powers. Likewise, every man's form and body is not the real man; it is merely a symbol and personification of the character and attributes of the real man, a form of matter in which the thoughts of the real man have found their external expression. The ancients knew these things; it is only the modern wiseacres who mistake the external illusions for internal truths, and the form for the principle. It is modern materialistic religion which has degraded the Universal Spirit into a limited being, and the great powers of nature into Christian saints."

We entered into a circular hall in the form of a temple. It had no windows, but received its light from a cupola of clear glass. High over our heads, below the cupola, was a large interlaced double triangle made of gold and surrounded by a snake biting its tail. In the midst of the room, and directly under that symbol, stood a round table with white marble top, in the centre of which was a smaller representation of the figure above, executed in silver. The walls were ornamented with bookcases, in which were a great number of books on alchemy. At one side of the room there was a kind of altar upon which stood a burning lamp. A couple of crucibles, a few bottles upon a side-table, and some armchairs completed the furniture of the room.

I looked around, expecting to see some furnaces, stoves, retorts, and other implements, such as are described in books on alchemy, but could see none. My instructor, reading my thoughts, laughingly said: "Did you expect to find here an apothecary's shop? You mistake, my friend. All this array of bottles and pots, of furnaces, stoves, retorts, mortars, filters, strainers, distilling, purifying, and re-fining apparatus, &c., described in books on alchemy, is nothing but nonsense, written to mislead the selfish and vicious, and to prevent them from prying into mysteries which they are not fit to receive. The true alchemist requires no ingredients for his processes, such as he could buy in a chemist's shop. He finds the materials which he needs within his own organisation. The highest processes of alchemy require no mechanical labour; they consist in the purification of the soul, and in transforming animal man into a divine being."

"But," said I, "did not the ancient al-chemists treat real metals and transform them into others of a higher order?"

To this Theodorus replied:

"The invisible principles of which the con-stitution of man is made up are called his *metals*, because they are more lasting and enduring than flesh and blood. The metals which are formed by his thoughts and desires will con-tinue to exist after the perishing elements con-stituting his physical body have been dissolved. Man's animal principles are the base metals of which his animal organisation consists; they must be changed into nobler metals by transforming his vices into virtue, until they pass through *all* colours and turn into the gold of pure spirituality. To accomplish this it is necessary that the grossest elements in his astral form should die and putrefy, so that the light of the spirit penetrate through the hard shell and call the inner man into life and activity."

" Then," I said, " all those alchemical prescriptions which we find in the books are only to be taken in a figurative sense, and have nothing to do with material substances, such as salt, sulphur, mercury, &c."

"Not exactly so," answered the Adept. " There are no hard lines separating the various kingdoms in nature, and the actions of laws manifested in one kingdom find their analogies in other kingdoms. The processes taking place in the spiritual planes are also taking place in in the astral and material planes, subject, of course, to such modifications as are imposed by the conditions existing upon these planes. Nature is not, as your scientists seem to believe, an agglomeration of fundamentally different objects and elements ; nature is a whole, and everything in the organism acts and is acted on by every other thing contained therein. This is a fact which the ancient alchemists knew, and which the modern chemists would do well to remember; for we find already in the book of *Sohar* the following passage, which I advise you to note down in your book, so that you will not forget it : *Everything that exists upon the Earth has its ethereal counterpart above the Earth* (that is to say, in the inner realm), *and there is nothing, however insignificant it may appear in the world, which is not depending on something higher* (or more interior); *so that if the lower part acts, its presiding higher part reacts upon it.*"

"It has been taught by the ancients," I interjected, "that man is a little world, constituted in a manner similar to the big world, which he inhabits."

"This is true," said the Adept ; "but you should not merely know it as a theory, but realise it. Within yourself is contained the universe with all its powers, heaven and hell, angels and devils, and all the kingdoms with their inhabitants, and you may call them into life at your pleasure. You are the god and creator within your own universe. You continually people that world with forms, coming into existence by your thoughts, and you infuse them with your life by the power of will. In each human being are contained germinally the essences which constitute the mineral, vegetable, animal, or human kingdom ; in each man are contained powers which may be developed into a tiger, a snake, a hog, a dragon, into a sage or a villain, into an angel or devil, into an Adept or a God. Those elements which are made to grow and to be developed will become the man's *alter ego* and constitute his "self." Look at the double interlaced triangle over your head ; it represents the Macrocosm with all the forces contained therein, the interpenetration and union of Spirit and Matter, within the never-ending circle of eternity. Look at the smaller symbol upon the table before you ; it represents the same elements within the constitution of Man. If you can bring the double interlaced triangles existing within your own body into harmony with those existing in the Universe, the powers of nature will be yours, and you will be able to guide and control them."

I thought of the nature of the many different ingredients necessary to make an alchemical experiment, and of the manner in which they must be mixed ; but Theodorus perceived my thought and replied :

"The universal process, by which all the processes of life take place, is the unfoldment of Life. He who can guide and control the power of life is an alchemist. He can create new forms and increase the substance of those forms. The chemist creates nothing new ; he merely forms new combinations of the substances in his possession; the alchemist causes the substance to attract corresponding elements from the invisible storehouse in nature, and to increase. The chemist deals with matter in which the principle of life is inactive, that is to say, in which it manifests itself merely as mechanical or chemical energy; the alchemist deals with the principle of life, and causes living forms to come into existence. The chemist may transform sulphur into invisible gas and cause that gas to become sulphur again, and the sulphur obtained at the end of the experiment will be just as much in quantity as it was at the beginning; but the gardener who puts a seed in the ground, and prepares the conditions necessary for that seed to grow into a tree, is an alchemist because he calls something into existence which did not exist ready-made in the seed, and out of one seed he may thus obtain a thousand seeds of the same kind."

"But," I objected, "it is said that the Rosicrucians possessed the power to turn iron, silver, or mercury into gold. Surely there is no gold in pure silver or mercury; how, then, could they cause something to grow which did not exist?"

The Adept smiled, and said: "Through your lips speaks the learned ignorance of your modern civilisation, which cannot see the truth, because it has created a mountain of misconceptions and scientific prejudices which now stand between itself and the truth. Let me then tell you once more that *Nature is a Unity,* and that consequently each particle of matter, even the smallest, is a part of nature in which the possibilities of the whole are hidden. Each speck of dust may under favourable conditions develop into a universe in which all the elements existing in nature can be found. The reason why your scientists are unable to comprehend this truth is because their fundamental doctrines about the constitution of matter and energy are entirely wrong. Your Dualism in theology has been the cause of untold misery, creating a continual quarrel between God and the Devil; your Polytheism in science blinds the eyes and obstructs the judgment of the learned, and keeps them in ignorance. What do you know about the attributes of primordial matter? What do you know about the difference between matter and force? All the so-called "simple substances" known to your science are originally grown out of primordial matter. But this primordial matter is a Unity; it is only *One.* Consequently each particle of this primordial matter must be able to grow under certain

conditions into gold, under other conditions to
produce iron, under others mercury, &c.   This
is what the ancient alchemists meant when
they said that each of the seven metals contains
the seeds of the other seven ; and they also
taught that, for the purpose of transmuting one
body into another, the body to be transmuted
would have to be reduced first into its *Prima
Materia*.

"But," he continued, "I see that you are
anxious to have the truth of these doctrines
demonstrated by an experiment; let us then
see whether it is possible that we can make
gold grow out of its *seed*."

Without rising from the big armchair in
which Theodorus was seated, he then directed
me to take one of the crucibles upon the table,
to see that it was empty, and to put it upon
a tripod over the flame burning upon the altar.
I did as directed.   He then said : "Now take
some of the silver pieces which you have in
your pocket, and throw them into the crucible."
I took seven pieces which I had with me, and
did as he said.   After a few minutes they
began to melt, and, as I saw the silver in the
crucible had become fluid, I told the Adept
that it was molten.   He then indicated a small
bottle containing some red powder, which stood
upon the table, and requested me to take some

of that red powder and to throw it into the crucible. There was a little silver spoon lying upon the table, and with this I took what seemed to be about one or two grains of the red powder from the bottle, and was going to throw it into the crucible, but Theodorus stopped me, saying that this was too much powder, and it should not be wasted. He told me to throw the powder back into the bottle and to wipe the spoon with a piece of paper, and then to throw the paper into the crucible. The quantity of powder which adhered to the spoon after I had returned the former to the bottle was so little as to be hardly visible; nevertheless, I did as he told me, and threw the little piece of paper upon the molten silver. Immediately the paper burned, and the molten metal began to foam and to rise, so that I was afraid that it would run over the sides of the crucible; but each bubble burst as it reached the top, and exhibited a variety of the most beautiful colours.

This play lasted for about fifteen minutes, when the boiling ceased, and the foaming mass sank back to the bottom of the crucible. Theodorus noticed that it had become quiet; he directed me to take the crucible from the fire and to pour the contents upon a marble slab. I did as he told me, and directly the mass became solid, and appeared to be the finest gold.

"Take this gold with you," said Theodorus, "and let it be examined, so that you will be convinced that you have not been the victim of an hallucination."

I was very much astonished, and I thought how much our people would give to become acquainted with the secret of this red powder. I desired to ask the Adept how this powder could be prepared, but I did not dare to ask the question aloud, because I was afraid that Theodorus would think I desired to know the secret for the purpose of enriching myself. But the Adept saw my thought, and said:

"The secret of how this red powder is prepared cannot be explained to men until they become more spiritual; because it is a secret whose knowledge must be practically acquired. How can we teach mankind to employ powers which they do not possess, and of which they do not even know the existence? Nevertheless, the germs of these powers are contained in a latent condition within the organism of every human being.

"It would be foolish to suppose that gold could be made out of any other substance than gold; but every substance contains the germ of gold in its own primordial state.

"In the alchemical laboratory of nature, iron-pyrites and other substances produce gold in the course of ages, because the principle of gold contained in their primordial element grows by the action of the life-principle of nature, and becomes visible gold. This process, which it may require unconscious nature millions of years to accomplish, can be accomplished by nature in a few minutes if her will-power is guided by the spiritual consciousness and intelligence of the Adept. It is as impossible to make gold grow out of anything containing no gold as it is impossible to make an apple tree grow out of a cherry stone. But if we wish to see an apple tree grow out of a seed we do not insert it in a hole bored into a rock, but we select a proper piece of soil where it can grow by the aid of sunlight and moisture. Likewise, if we desire gold to grow out of the 'seed' or *principle* of gold, we must add the proper soil which it requires; and this 'soil' is furnished by the red powder, which contains the life-principle for the production of gold. Know that there is no 'dead' substance in the universe, and that even a stone or a metal contains life in a latent form. If the life-principle within such a substance becomes active, this substance will begin to form and to produce the various

H

colours which you saw in the crucible. If the mass were cold and solid, the power of life would be slow to penetrate below the surface of the metal; nevertheless, the transmutation would gradually take place; but in the molten mass the life-giving substance becomes thoroughly mixed with the metal, ebullition takes place, and the transmutation is quickly performed.

"Why should growth and development and transmutation of form be possible only in the vegetable and animal kingdom? It is equally possible in the mineral kingdom; the only difference is that in the former it takes place within a sufficiently short period of time, so as to come within the observation of man; while in the latter these processes take place very slowly, and many generations of men may pass away before any progress in the growth of metals can be observed.

"The seed for the production of plants grows in the plants themselves; the seed for the production of animals grows in the animals; the 'seed' for the production of metals rests in the metals. It is not sufficient merely to melt a metal, to make it grow; it must be made subject to the power of life. This is done by the addition of the red powder, of which an almost imperceptible quantity is sufficient to cause the growth of a great quantity of gold. The few atoms of powder which you used were enough and to spare to transmute your silver, as you will see if you now examine your gold, which has not absorbed all of the red powder which adhered to the paper."

I looked at the gold, which had now become cold enough to be handled, and, indeed, upon its surface there were some little red pearls like rubies, which seemed to indicate that they were parts of the red powder which had not been absorbed by the molten mass.

"Master!" I exclaimed, "teach me this secret, and I promise you that I will never use the knowledge obtained for any selfish purpose whatever. I have learned enough of occultism to know that worldly possessions and riches are useless for the purpose of spiritual development, and that they are in truth the greatest obstacles which can be put in the way of those who desire to progress. I only desire to know the truth for the sake of the truth, and not for the purpose of obtaining any selfish advantage. Teach me these secrets, and I will forget my own self, and devote my life to benefit the universal brotherhood of humanity."

"Very well," answered the Adept. "I will do all I can to show you the way, but you must do your own walking. To teach you the secret of how to make gold is identical with teaching you all the secrets of the constitution of nature, and of its counterpart, the microcosm of man. This cannot be done in a few hours, or within a few days, and it would be against the rules of our order to retain you here longer than after sunset. But to enable you to study this science of alchemy, I will lend you a book which you may read and study; and if you keep your intuitional faculties open and your mind unclouded, I will be invisibly near you and assist you to understand the meaning of the secret symbols contained therein."

With these words Theodorus handed me a book containing a number of coloured plates with symbols and signs. It was an old book, and its title was "The Secret Symbols of the Rosicrucians of the Sixteenth and Seventeenth Centuries."

"The size of the book," continued the Adept, "renders it rather inconvenient for you to carry it on your descent from the mountain, but I will send it to your hotel at the village, where you will find it on your arrival."

I thanked the Adept, and looked once more at the mysterious book. I glanced at the titles of the pages, and saw that they treated about the greatest of mysteries, of the Macrocosm and

Microcosm, of Time and Eternity, of Occult Numbers, the Four Elements, the Trinity of All, of Regeneration, Alchemy, Philosophy, and Cabala; it was indeed a book on *Universal Science.*

" If you practically understand the contents of this book," said Theodorus, " you will not merely know how to produce gold out of the baser metals, which is one of the lowest, most insignificant, and comparatively worthless parts of our art, but you will know the mystery of the Rose and the Cross ; you will know how to come into possession of the *Philosopher's Stone* and the *Universal Panacea,* which renders those who possess it immortal. You will then not merely know how to direct the processes of life, so as to make pearls and diamonds and precious stones grow, but you will know how to make a man out of an animal, and a god out of a man. This last alchemical process is the one thing which is needed, and in comparison all other arts are merely playthings for children. What will it serve us to run after illusions, which will vanish in time, if we can obtain within ourselves that which is eternal and real ? "

I asked the Adept whether I would be permitted to show that book to others, or to have it copied and printed ; upon which he replied :

"There are at present few people in the world who would be able to comprehend this book to its fullest extent; but there are some who desire to know the truth, and for the sake of these few you may risk to throw pearls before the swine. The symbols contained in these pages must be not merely seen and studied with the intellect, they must also be grasped by the spirit. To make this plain to you, know that each occult symbol and sign, from a mere point up to the double-interlaced Triangle, to the Rose and the Cross, has three significations. The first is the exoteric meaning, which is easily understood; the second is the esoteric or secret signification, which may be intellectually explained; the deepest and most mysterious one is the third, the spiritual meaning, which cannot be explained, but which must be spiritually experienced within yourself. This practical, internal experience is arrived at by the power of intuition, or the faculty by which the soul feels the presence of things which one cannot see with the bodily senses. If a person once feels interior things with his heart, sees them by his internal sight, and understands their attributes, then such a person has become illuminated, and is practically an Adept.

"As the number *Three* grows out of the *One*, likewise the *Seven* grows out of the *Three*;

because by a combination of three numbers or letters four complications arise, forming with the original Three the number Seven; and thus there are not merely three, but seven explanations of each symbol. You see, therefore, that the matter is very complicated, and requires deep study. Nor would it benefit you if I were to explain to you all the various meanings of these symbols; for you must learn to realise that you yourself are a symbol. These symbols represent the mysteries of the universe and of man. You are that universe, you are the man, and these things are representing yourself. What good would the explanations do to you if you do not realise that they are true?"

"But," I interposed, "if this is so, it will be useless to read any such books."

"Those who know these things themselves," said Theodorus, "do not need them, and those who do need them do not understand them. Books of that kind are like mirrors in which a man sees the things reflected which are existing in him. A monkey stands before a looking-glass and sees his own image, but he thinks it is another monkey aping his motions. If you know the contents of a book, describing a truth, you only know the description but not the very truth itself. You may know the contents of the Bible by heart from beginning to end, together with all the commentaries, and still not realise the truth of one iota of it. Self is the man. That which he finds out by his own experience, that he *knows*, and nothing more.

"When I was an inhabitant of your world, I had many a hard rub with your doctors of medicine and of divinity, because they lived upon the ignorance of the people, and the more I enlightened the latter, the less flattering grew the bread-and-butter prospects of the former. I usually found that the more learned your doctors were, the more did they lose their own common sense. I live here in peace, and care little about their disputations and argumentations; but I take occasionally a glance at the world, and I do not see much change for the better."

"Nevertheless," I said, "you will agree that science has made a great deal of progress since those days?"

"True," he answered, "she has progressed in some things and retrograded in others. She has made many inventions to increase the physical comforts of man and to gratify his desires; but in proportion as man's desires have been gratified, they have also grown, and new necessities have been created. Many of your most useful inventions, however, have not been made by the help, but rather in spite of the opposition, of your professional scientists.

"Moreover, if the psychical faculties of man were developed, many of your most useful inventions would be perfectly useless; they would be displaced by far better methods, in the same sense as bows and arrows have become useless since the invention of gunpowder and guns. You are very proud of your railroads and telegraphs, but of what use are they to a man who is able to travel with the velocity of thought from one place to another, however distant that place may be. Learn to chain the elemental spirits of nature to the chariot of your science, and you may mount like an eagle and ride through the air."

"I should be very glad," I said, "if you would inform me how a person can travel with the velocity of thought from one place to another. It seems to me that the weight of the physical body would present an insurmountable impediment."

"Neither would psychically developed man need to take that cumbrous form along on such travels," answered Theodorus. "What or who is Man? Is he that semi-animal mechanism, which eats, drinks, and walks, and wastes nearly half of its life in unconscious sleep; that mass of bones and muscles, of blood and sensitive nerves, which hinders the free movements of the spirit who is chained to it; or is *the man* that invisible something which thinks and feels, and knows that it exists?"

I said: "Undoubtedly the real man is the thinking principle in man."

"If you admit this," answered the Adept, "you will also agree that the real man is in that place and locality wherein he thinks and perceives; in other words, he is there where his consciousness exists. Thinking is a faculty of the mind, and not a faculty of the physical body. It is not my brain which thinks; but I myself do my thinking by means of my brain. Wherever our mind exercises that faculty, there is our true habitation; whether our physical form is there, too, is a circumstance which need not concern us any more than it would concern us to carry a warm and heavy coat which we are accustomed to wear in winter along with us while we are making a summer excursion. Thinking is a faculty of the mind, and Mind is universal. If we learn to think independently of our physical brain, we may as well exercise that faculty in one place of the universe as in another, without taking our physical body along."

"But," I objected, "how can a universal and therefore unorganised principle think, without using for that purpose an organised brain?"

"Short-sighted mortal!" exclaimed Theodorus. "Who says that Mind is without an organisation? Who has so little judgment as to suppose that the highest organised living and conscious principle in the universe is without an organisation, if even the inferior kingdoms upon the face of the earth, such as crystal, plant, and animal, cannot exist without an organisation? Surely the air does not think; it has no firm organisation; but the Universal Mind is not air, nor is it empty space; it has nothing in common with either, except its being everywhere present. It is the highest organised principle in the universe.

"Inferior man, in whom the consciousness of his higher spiritual self has not awakened, cannot think without the aid of the physical brain; he cannot experience a consciousness which he does not yet possess; he cannot exercise a faculty which is merely latent within his organisation. But the man who has awakened to the consciousness of his higher self, whose life has been concentrated into his higher principles, which exist independently of the physical form, constitutes a *spiritual* centre of consciousness, which does not require the physical brain to think, any more than you require the use of your hands and feet for the purpose of thinking. If a person in a somnambulic condition travels in spirit to a distant place and reports what he has seen there, and his observations are afterwards verified, must we not conclude that he has been at that place, and would it be reasonable to suppose that he has taken his physical brain with him and left the empty skull behind? How absurd is such an idea; but verily its absurdity does not surpass that of your suggestion, that the universal mind is without an organisation."

I was somewhat confused at having inconsiderately expressed an opinion about a subject of which I could not know anything, and the Adept, noticing my regret, continued in a mild manner : " If you desire to know the organisation of nature, study your own constitution, not merely in its physical, anatomical, and physiological aspect, but especially in its psychological aspect. Study what may be called the physiology of your soul. If your foot were not an organised substance intimately connected with your brain by means of the nerves and the spinal cord, you would never be able to feel any sensation in your foot ; the latter might be burned or amputated, and you would not be aware of it unless you should see its destruction. You do not think with your foot, you think with your brain ; or, to express it more correctly, you think by means of your brain. But if you were more spiritually developed, you would be able to sink your thought and consciousness from your brain down into your feet, or into any other part of your body, and, so to say, live in that part and be entirely unconscious of any other part. It has already come to the comprehension of some of your more advanced scientists that sensation and consciousness may be withdrawn from any part of the body, either by an effort of the will and imagination of the person who undertakes the experiment, or by the aid of the will and imagination of a ' magnetizer ' or ' mesmerizer.' In the same manner the opposite thing can be done, and a person may concentrate himself, so to say, in any part of his own organism, or in any part of the great organism of nature with which he is intimately and inseparably, although invisibly, connected. A man who believes that he exists independently of nature and separated from it, labours under a great delusion. The fundamental doctrine of occultism is that nature is only one, and that all beings in nature are intimately connected together, and that everything in nature acts upon every other thing therein. The feeling of isolation and separateness existing in individuals is only caused by the illusion of form. Man's form is not man; it is merely a state of matter in which man for the time being exists, and which is continually subject to change. It may be compared to an image in a mirror in which the character of man is imperfectly reflected, and although it differs from the image in a mirror in so far as it is temporarily endowed or infused with life, sensation, and consciousness, nevertheless it is nothing else than an image; for life, sensation, and consciousness do not belong to the form; they are functions of the invisible but real man who forms a part of the invisible organism of nature, and whose mind is a part of the universal mind, and who, therefore, if he once realises his true character and learns to know his own powers, may concentrate his consciousness in any place, within or beyond his physical form, and see, feel, and understand what takes place in such a locality."

"These ideas," I said, "are so grand that I am not yet fully able to grasp them; but I fear that they will never be accepted by our scientists, who cannot see beyond the narrow systems which they themselves have created."

"True," answered the Adept; "they will not

be accepted or understood by our present generation of scientists; but they will be known in
the future to those who are not merely learned,
but *wise*, as they were known to the wise men
of the past. Ignorance and self-conceit are twin-
brothers; and it flatters man's vanity to believe
that he is something superior to and different
from the rest; and the more a man is learned in
superficial science, the more does he believe in
his own imaginary superiority and separateness.
The consciousness of the great majority of intelligent people in our intellectual age is nearly
all concentrated within their brains; they live,
so to say, entirely in the top-storey of their
houses. But the brain is not the most important part of the house in which man resides.
The centre of life is the heart; and if consciousness does not take its residence in the centre
of life, it will become separate from life, and
finally cease to exist. Let those who desire to
develop spiritually attempt to think with their
hearts, instead of merely studying with their
brains. Let them attempt to sink day after
day their power of thought down to the centre
of life in the heart, until their consciousness is
firmly established there. At first they will see
nothing but darkness; but, if they persevere in
their efforts, they will behold a light at that
centre which illuminates the mind. This in-

extinguishable light will send its rays to the brain and carry them as far as the stars ; and in it they may see the past, the present, and the future.

"The greatest mysteries in nature are by no means difficult to understand, if we only prefer to look at them instead of looking at our own delusions. The grandest ideas are easy to grasp, if we merely prefer to grasp them instead of holding on to our fancies. Man's mind is like a mirror in which the ideas floating in the universal mind are reflected, comparable to a tranquil lake in which you may see the true images of the passing clouds. If the surface of the lake is disturbed, the images become distorted; if the water becomes muddy, the reflections cease altogether. Likewise, if the mind of man is in a tranquil state and clear of foreign elements, he will reflect the grandest and noblest ideas existing within the world of mind. If we desire to think reasonably, we should allow the goddess of Reason to do her thinking within our brain ; but if we attempt to be wiser than Reason, our mind becomes filled with our own fancies and those which we have acquired from others, and we cannot see the truth as it is, but we see it as we imagine it to be.

"This truth you will find symbolically or

allegorically represented in all the principal mythologies and religious systems of the world. It is the old story of the 'Fall of Man.' As long as man remained in a state of purity— that is to say, as long as his will and imagination were one and identical with the will and the imagination of the spiritual creative power in nature — he knew the truth and was all-powerful; but when he began to think and to imagine in a way different from that universal power, he lost sight of the truth and could see only his own fancies. If man wants to see the truth again, he must give up his own way of reasoning and let Reason act in him. But you may as well ask a miser to give up the treasure which he has collected and hoarded during a lifetime as to ask a modern scientist or philosopher to give up his own crooked ways. I see in your heart a desire to establish a secret society; but let me warn you that if you attempt to accomplish this by appealing to those who are clever and cunning, vainglorious and proud of their own attainments, full of ambition and anxious to come into possession of occult or magical powers for the purpose of gratifying their scientific curiosity or to employ them for the fulfilment of some selfish desire, you will certainly fail; for it is written : "Whosoever hath, to him shall be given and he shall have more in abundance, but whosoever hath not, from him shall be taken away even that he hath."

"I know that quotation," I answered, "but its meaning is not quite clear to me."

"It means," replied Theodorus, "that to him who has the love of wisdom in his heart, abundant light will be given; but from him who is filled with selfish desires, what little understanding he has will be taken away."

"I acknowledge," I said, "that I have been thinking of finding means to establish a society, or a school for spiritual development, where those who desire to progress might be able to spend their energies for the purpose of that which is useful and lasting, instead of being forced to run after the illusions of the world. I have been mentally seeking for a place in a solitude where the members of such a society might lead an interior life. I should like to establish a theosophical monastery, where we could live like yourself, surrounded by all the grandeur, sublimity, and stillness of nature, escape the servitude of fashionable society, and step on the path to adeptship. But surely I could not think of selecting our members from the ranks of the uneducated and ignorant."

"Select them among those who are strong and virtuous," answered Theodorus, "and your choice will be well made. Choose those who have overcome preconceived opinions and pre-judices; select them among those who have no desire to obtain knowledge for their own per-sonal benefit and do not wish to shine, but to let the light grow within themselves. Such persons are very rare; but if you find any, and if they join you in your efforts, you will soon have the most enlightened society in the world. That which is to-day called learning and education is merely a very laborious method of acquiring a little superficial knowledge which mankind is forced to adopt because they do not know how to develop their spiritual perception. If this method were taught and practised, real know-ledge would soon occupy the place of mere learning, certainty the place of belief, conviction the place of opinion, true faith the place of creed. If the inhabitants of your proposed convent were pure-minded men and women, great souls and living mirrors in which Divine Wisdom could be reflected without any adulteration, such a monastery would be the greatest ornament of the world. Such centres of spiritual intelligence would be like suns of the first magnitude on the mental horizon of the world. One such centre would be sufficient to illuminate the world with its wisdom and to send its intellectual rays to the utmost limits of the planet."

" And what is to hinder the establishment of such a centre of intelligence ? " I asked.

"Nothing but the imperfections of man and the abundance of his selfish desires. There are two sources from which the obstacles arise that are in the way of those who desire to attain self-knowledge and immortality. One class of obstacles arises from man's interior self, the other from the external conditions in which he lives. The internal obstacles are caused by his acquired scientific or theological prejudices and misconceptions regarding the constitution of man, and by the living elemental forces active within the animal principle in his constitution. As they are fed and grow strong by external influences, they manifest themselves in various ways, producing animal impulses, and in combination with the intellectual acquirements they grow into the more dangerous class of vices, such as ambition, vanity, greed, intolerance, selfishness, &c. Each of these animal elements, or *Elementals*, may grow into an intellectual but unreasonable being, and finally constitute the very *alter ego* of man. Man may have a great many such false *egos* within him, until perhaps one of these overmasters the others and becomes a king in the realm of his soul. Each such "self" absorbs a share of the life and consciousness of the man in whose soul it exists, and may finally even occupy all space within his intellectual sphere, so as to paralyse reason or drive it away. The world is crowded with such intellectual or semi-intellectual Elementals in human shape, in whom reason has been paralysed to a greater or lesser extent. You see them every day in the streets, in the pulpit, the forum, in the halls of learning, as well as upon the market-place. Man's principal object in life should be to keep the realm of his mind free from such intruders, so that the king Reason may rule therein without being impeded. His duty is to fight the herculean battle with those animal and intellectual Elementals, so that they will become servants of the king, and not become his masters. Can this be accomplished if all our energies are continually employed on the outward plane; if we are never at home within ourselves; if we are continually engaged with the illusions of life, either in the pursuit of sensual gratification or entirely absorbed in scientific pursuits, which tend to give us knowledge of outward things but convey no knowledge of self? Can we expect to accumulate our energy and employ it at the centre within ourselves, if we continually spend it at the periphery ? Can we hope to be able to waste all our power, and at the same time to be able to retain it ? An affirmative answer would be as irrational as unscientific."

VII

THE HIGHER LIFE

It would be too tedious to some of our readers if I were to report all the instructions that were given to me by my kind guide Theodorus, who, for all I know, may have been known as the celebrated Theophrastus Paracelsus during his life in the physical body. I do not, however, feel myself justified in omitting to tell what he said in regard to the importance of practising self-control and developing firmness of character and individuality. Previously to my visit to the Rosicrucian convent I had been made to believe that occultism and mysticism were things only for dreamers; adapted to persons living continually in the clouds, enjoying their superstitions and vagaries by building castles in the air; but now, I found, that self-reliance is a most necessary quality for a disciple of this sacred science, and that no science can be more exact than the one based upon our own exact spiritual knowledge and realised within our own soul. Thus Theodorus said :

"A power to become strong at a centre must be directed towards the centre; for it is only by resistance that it can accumulate and become strong. A king who goes away from his kingdom and leaves it without protection may find other rulers there when he attempts to return. To become conquerors over nature we must fight our own battles, and not wait until nature fights them for us. The more the animal elements within man's constitution are stimulated into life and activity by the temptations coming from the external world through the avenues of the senses, the hotter will be the battle, and the stronger will man's power grow if he successfully resists. This is the battle which the great Gautama Buddha fought and from which he came out victorious, because he was overshadowed by the *Bo-tree* of Wisdom.

"I will attempt to give you a rational explanation of the effects of inward concentration, to show you how you may become a creator of your own world.

"According to the teachings of the sages the Universal Spirit called the world into existence by the power of His own thought. All great religions speak of a divine Triunity, according to Christianity called the Father, the Son, and the Holy Ghost. The will or intention is the Father, the thought or idea the Son, and the creative power of the Father acting through the Son is the Holy Ghost. By this power the thoughts of the Father become manifest, and thus visible objective worlds are called into existence."

"But," said I, "where does the Father find the material or substance to render these thoughts visible and objective?"

"Within Himself," answered my guide, and, looking at me as if to make sure that I understood the meaning of what he said, he continued : *"Allah il Allah*, says the Mohammedan ; God is God, and there is nothing beside Him. He is the All; matter and motion and space, consciousness, intelligence, wisdom, spirit, substance, energy, darkness, and light. The worlds are His outspoken thoughts ; but there is nothing outside of Himself of which He might think, He being the All, including and penetrating everything. Thus everything exists within Him, who is the life and soul of all things. In Him we live and move and have our being, and without Him we are nothing.

"Man is the god and creator of his own little world, and therefore similar processes take place when a person, by the power of introspection, directs his thoughts towards his own centre of consciousness within his 'heart.' Now this activity going towards the centre could never of itself have created an external world, because the external world belongs to the periphery, and it requires a centrifugal power to call it into existence. The introspective activity of the Mind is a centripetal power, and could therefore not act from the centre towards the periphery. But you know that every action is followed by a reaction. The centripetal power, finding resistance at the centre, returns and evolves a centrifugal activity, and this centrifugal power is called Imagination. This *Soul-energy* is the medium between the centre and the periphery, between Spirit and Matter, between the Creator and His creations, between God and Nature, or whatever names you may choose to give to them. The Soul-consciousness is the product of the centrifugal activity of the Mind, put into action by the centripetal activity of the Will.

"If these plain facts, expressed in plain language, without any scientific jargon, without circumlocutions, philosophical intricacies and modern gibberish, are comprehensible to you, all you have to do is to apply it to yourself. If you direct the power of your mind inwardly towards your centre, instead of letting it fly off at a tangent, the resistance which it finds at the centre will cause a reaction, and the stronger the centripetal power which you apply, the stronger will be the centrifugal power created; in other words, the stronger will your *Soul* become, and, as she grows strong, her invisible, but nevertheless material, substance will penetrate your physical, visible body, and serve to transform it into a higher kind. Thus you may at the end become all *Soul*, and have no gross physical body. But long before that time arrives you will be able to act upon matter by the power of your soul, to cure your own bodily ills and those of other people, and to do many wonderful things, even at distances far away from your visible form; for the activity of the soul is not limited by the circumference of the physical form, but radiates far into the sphere of the Universal Mind."

I told Theodorus that these ideas were as yet too grand and too new to me, to be grasped immediately; but that I would attempt to remember them and to meditate about them in the future.

"You will do well if you do so," said the Adept, "and I will take care that they remain in your memory."

"If the doctrines of the sages are true," I

replied, "it would seem that the vast majority of our thinkers are continually thinking the wrong way ; because they are engaged all their lives in prying into the manifestations of life on the outward plane, and do not seem to care a straw about what is taking place within the inner life of the soul."

"Therefore," answered Theodorus, "they will perish with their illusions ; and the Bible is right in saying that the ways of the worldly-wise are foolishness in the eyes of the Eternal.

"What will it serve you, if your head is full of speculations about the details of the phenomenal illusions of life, and you become a senile imbecile in your old age ? What will it serve you, roaming about the world and gratifying your curiosity in regard to its details, when, after that world has vanished, they for ever disappear from your memory ? Perhaps it would be better for the learned if they knew less of scientific theories and had more soul knowledge. It would be better if they had fewer theories and more experience. If they were to employ, for instance, some of their time and energy for the development of the spiritual power of clairvoyance, instead of spending it to find out the habits of some species of African monkey, they would fare better by it. If they were to obtain the power to heal the sick by the touch of their hands, instead of seeking new methods to poison humanity by inoculations of injurious substances, humanity would be the gainer. There are thousands of people who work hard all their lives, without accomplishing anything which is really useful or enduring. There are thousands who labour intellectually or mechanically to perform work which had better be left undone. There are vastly more people engaged in undermining and destroying the health of man than in curing his ills, more engaged in teaching error than in teaching the truth, more trying to find that which is worthless than that which is of value ; they live in dreams and their dreams will vanish ; they run after money, and the money will remain while they themselves perish and die.

"The obstacles which arise from the external world are intimately connected with those from the inner world, and cannot be separated ; because external temptations create inward desires, and inward desires call for external means for gratification. There are many people who do not crave for the illusions of life, but who have not the strength to resist them ; they have a desire to develop spiritually and to gain immortality, but employ all of their time and energy for the attainment of worthless things, instead of using it to dive down into the depths of the soul to search for the priceless pearl of wisdom. Thousands of people have not the moral courage to break loose from social customs, ridiculous habits, and foolish usages, which they inwardly abhor, but to which they nevertheless submit because they are customs and habits to act against which is considered to be a social crime. Thus thousands sacrifice their immortality to the stupid goddess of fashion.

"Who dares to break loose from the bondage imposed upon him by the fashion which at present dominates religious thought? Who has the courage to incur the sneers of the imbecile, the ridicule of the ignorant, the laughter of the fool, and gain thereby a light of whose existence those who live in eternal darkness know nothing? The vast majority of people drown the voice of reason and dance with the fool. Rather than have their vanity suffer, they allow the spirit to starve; rather than be crucified and rise into immortal life, they submit to the galling chain; they lose their appreciation of liberty, and, becoming used to their chains, begin to love them and impose them upon others.

"I am not a believer in the total depravity of human nature; I know that man's animal energies, on account of their inherent instinctive efforts for the preservation of their existence, are opposed to the development of his higher principles, because the life of the higher involves the death of the lower ; but I also know that in each human being is contained a power for good, which may be made to develop if the proper conditions are given. There are elements of good and elements of evil in every man, and it depends on ourselves which class we desire to develop. From a cherry stone nothing can grow but a cherry tree, from a thistle seed nothing else than a thistle ; but man is a constellation of powers in which all kinds of seeds are contained ; you may make him grow to be a hog or a tiger, an angel or a devil, a sage or a fool, according to your own pleasure.

"The continual rush after more money, more comfort, more pleasure, after we already possess all we require, which characterises our present civilisation, is not necessarily a sign of viciousness and moral depravity ; but it is rather caused by the instinctive impulse, inherent in the constitution of man, to reach some higher and better condition, which expresses itself on the mundane plane. Man intuitively knows that, no matter how rich in money or fame he may be, he has not yet reached a state in which he will be contented to rest ; he knows that he must still keep on striving for something, but he does not know what that something is. Not knowing the higher life, he strives for more of those things which the lower life affords. Thus we may see a bug or a butterfly falling into a lake, and in its vain efforts to save itself from drowning swimming away from the shore, because it does not know in which direction the means for salvation exist. The curse of the world and the root of all evil is ignorance. The curse of man is his ignorance of his higher nature and final destiny, and the efforts of a true system of religion and science ought to be above all to remove this stupidity.

"But it is also true that ignorance and conceit are closely connected together, and that the ignorant hate him who is wiser than they. If one man, knowing more about the requirements of his nature, and desirous to employ all his energies for the attainment of a higher state, were to dare to assert his manhood and to rebel against the chains of fashion, could he continue to live unmolested in his community? and if he were to emigrate to another, would he not be exposed there to the same troubles? He would still come in contact with men who hated freedom because they were educated in chains, who would misunderstand him, suspect his motives, and persecute him; and woe to him if he had any human failings upon which the snake of slander could fasten its poison fangs. Wherever darkness exists, there exists abhorrence of light.

Wherever ignorant man enters, there enter his imperfections. Wherever ignorance resides, there are her attending angels, suspicion, envy, and fear. Would it not be more within the scope of a true science to enlighten man about his higher nature, than to dig for worms in the bowels of the material plane?

"That which is almost impossible to accomplish by the unaided efforts of a single individual, may often easily be accomplished by the co-operation of many, and this law seems to prevail in all departments of nature. If a sufficient number of people were determined to retire from the harlequin stage of the world and to turn away from the tomfooleries of a fashionable existence, they might, if they could harmonise with each other, form a power sufficiently strong to repel the attacks of the monster which would devour them all if they were separated and unaided by each other. Those who are not yet progressed far on the ladder of evolution need those who are upon a higher step to assist them on their upward way, and the higher ones need the lower for their support, in the same sense as a rock needs a solid ground to rest upon and maintain its position.

"There have been at previous times, as there are now, numerous people who became convinced that there is a higher and inner life, and who

K

desired to surround themselves with such conditions as were most favourable for its attainment.
Such people were not merely to be found in
Christian countries, but also among the 'heathen.'
Lamaseries and lodges, orders, monasteries, convents, and places of refuge have been established, where people might strive to attain a
higher life, unimpeded by the aggressions and
annoyances of the external world of illusions.
Their original purpose was beyond a doubt very
commendable. If in the course of time many
such institutions have become degraded and
lost their original character; if instead of being
places for the performance of the noblest and
most difficult kind of labour, they have become
places of refuge for the indolent, idle, and super-
stitious; it is not the fault of that principle
which first caused such institutions to be organised, but it is the consequence of the knowledge
of the higher nature of man and his powers
and destiny having been lost, and with the loss
of that knowledge, the means for the attainment, the original aim, was naturally lost and
forgotten.

"Such a degradation took place in Europe,
especially during and after the Middle Ages,
when, enriched by robberies and endowed by
dying thieves who wanted to buy salvation,
the clergy amassed great wealth and lived a

luxurious life, feasting on the fat of the land.
They then knew nothing more of the conditions
of a higher existence; they became centres of
attraction for the hypocrite and the idle. They
passed away their idle hours in apparently
pious amusements, and in striving to gain more
material wealth. Instead of being centres from
which blessings should spread over the country,
they became a plague to the land. They
robbed the rich, and, vampire-like, they sucked
the last drop of blood out of the poor. They
continued in this manner until the cup of their
crimes was full, when the great Reformation
caused the downfall of many and a certain
reform of the rest.

"There are still numerous convents existing
in Europe, and in America their number is on
the increase. The modern reformer, the socialist
and materialist, looks upon them with an evil
eye; but the unprejudiced observer will not
deny that some of them are doing a great deal
of good in their own way. Some have established schools, others opened hospitals; and
above all are the Sisters of Charity unsurpassed
in their usefulness in the care for the sick.
Thus some of these orders serve the noble purpose of benefiting humanity, and their usefulness could be increased a thousandfold if the
light of spiritual knowledge—the Holy Ghost,

to whom they pray—were to be permitted to descend upon their ranks.

"Do the religious orders as they are now fulfil their original purpose of raising man up into a higher and spiritual state of existence, or are they merely centres around which pious and benevolent people have collected who teach schools and nurse the sick—occupations which might perhaps equally well be performed without professing any particular creed? If the religious convents are calculated to develop true spirituality and to produce truly regenerated men and women, they will be the places where we may find some manifestation of spiritual powers; for a latent power which never manifests itself is of no use; it cannot exist in an active state without manifesting itself. Let us therefore be permitted to ask: Do the inhabitants of our convents consciously exercise any spiritual powers? Can they knowingly cure the sick by the touch of their hands? Are their inner senses sufficiently opened, so that they may see and hear, taste, smell, and feel things which are imperceptible to the senses of average man? Can they prophesy, with any degree of certainty, future events, except by the conclusions of logic? Are there any among them who have become Adepts? What do they actually know about the conditions required to enter a higher state of consciousness than that of ordinary mortals? What do they know about the means to enter adeptship and to obtain a conscious existence as souls? What do our monks and nuns know about the constitution of the human soul, and especially of those souls who are entrusted to their care? What are their experiences when in that higher state called ecstasy? If there is one among them who enters into a state of trance, or is levitated into the air, or able to produce a simple mediumistic phenomenon, do they know the occult causes which produce such effects, or is not such an occurrence considered to be an unexplainable or supernatural miracle?

"It is idle for the priests to assert that they can forgive sins, or that sins can be forgiven through them. If they do not possess any spiritual powers, we cannot believe that they are able to communicate them to others; and if they convey such powers to others, where are their effects to be seen? Do the ignorant become wise after having been baptized with water? Do those who have submitted to the ceremony of confirmation obtain firmness of faith? Does the sinner become innocent after having the load taken off from his conscience by means of absolution? Can

our clergymen change the laws of nature?
Can they by any external ceremony cause the
growth of an inner principle? or does he who
enters a church an animal, come out an animal
still?

"These are perplexing questions, and I would
not like to be understood as if I desired to
throw any discredit upon the motives of any
of the inhabitants of our convents and nun-
neries. I am personally acquainted with many
of them, and found them to be good and kind
and well-meaning people, without that priestly
pride and arrogance which unfortunately often
characterise the clergymen of the world; but
I believe that all the good which they do they
could perform as well, and even a great deal
better, if they were to undertake the study of
the soul, its organisation and functions, and if
they were qualifying themselves for that study.
They would then be able to develop consciously
those higher faculties which have spontaneously
developed among some of their members, who,
on account of such an unexpected and abnormal
development, were called miracle-workers or
saints.

"How can any one be a true spiritual guide
who has no spiritual powers, and who, perhaps,
does not even know that such powers exist?
What would you think of a surgeon who knew

nothing whatever of anatomy ? what of a
physician who did not know his patient ?
what of a blind painter, a deaf musician, an
imbecile mathematician ? What shall we think
of a physician of the soul who knows nothing
at all about the soul or its attributes, who
has never seen it, and is merely of the opinion
that it exists ? Have we not a right to doubt
the usefulness of such a physician, and exclaim
with Shakespeare—

"Throw physic to the dogs; I'll none of it"?

If the inhabitants of our convents and monasteries, instead of employing the time and
energy which they need for the performance
of their customary ceremonies, for the saying
of rosaries and the repetitions of litanies, &c.,
were to employ them for the purpose of acquiring self-knowledge, for the study of the
essential constitution of man and of nature,
and for the acquisition of spiritual power, their
usefulness might be extended to an enormous
degree. Their knowledge would be no longer
restricted to earthly things, but expand to
heaven ; they would not need to nurse the
sick, for they could cure them by the touch
of their hands ; they would not need to baptize
people with water, for they could baptize them
with the spirit of sanctity ; they would not

need to listen to confessions, for they would
be able to read the thoughts of the culprit.
Why should they not be able to do their
duties much better if they were wise instead
of ignorant; if they knew the truth instead
of blindly accepting a creed; if they had the
power to accomplish that which they now
expect an invisible and unknown power to
accomplish in response to their prayers? If
the public believe that there is one miracle-
working saint at a convent, do they not rush
there to receive his or her blessings? What
would be the fame of a convent composed
entirely of saints whose powers could not be
doubted?

"But how can monks and nuns acquire such
powers? How can they qualify themselves
for such a study? It has been said that it is
ten times more difficult to remove an old error
than to find a new truth; and there lies the
difficulty. A page which is already full of
writing will have to be cleaned before it can be
written upon again. They would have to purge
their minds of all dogmatism and sophistry
before they can see the light of truth; they
would have to become like children before they
can enter the kingdom of heaven within their
own souls. They would have to remove the
mountain of rubbish which has accumulated

in time in the vestibule of the temple, consisting of errors and superstitions, and of the corpses of forms from which the spirit has fled. Ages of ignorance have contributed to its growth, and it has become venerable by age. The inhabitants of the convent bare their heads and bend their knees when they approach that pile, and they do not dare to destroy it. To become wise, they would have to learn the true meaning of their own doctrines, symbols, and books, of which they at present merely know the outward form and the dead letter. They would have to form a much higher and nobler conception of God than to invest Him with the attributes of semi-animal man. They would have to base their moral doctrines upon the intrinsic dignity of the divine principle in man, instead of appealing to the selfish desires of man and to his fear of punishment, to induce him to seek his salvation.

"This may be accomplished in the far-distant future, but not at the present time. Ages and centuries may roll away before the sunlight of truth will penetrate through the thick veil of materialism and superstition which, like an icy crust, covers the true foundation of human religions. Look at the ice-fields of the Alps, covering the sides of the mountains, sometimes many miles in area. They extend in solid

blocks, perhaps more than a hundred feet thick,
down to the valley. They are the products
of centuries; and firm as the rock the ice
appears; and yet these rigid and apparently
immovable masses move and slowly change
from year to year. They grate the rocks upon
which they rest, and they throw out that which
is foreign. There may cracks and fissures be
seen at the top, and if, as happens sometimes,
a man falls into one of these fissures, his remains
will be found many years afterwards at the
foot of the glacier, below the field of ice, having
been spewed out by the same.

"Change, slow change, is going on everywhere in nature. Even in the most rigid and
orthodox religious systems, in the most be-
nighted hearts and heads, there is going on a
continual change. Already the doctrines which
were expounded in the pulpits of the Middle
Ages have been modified to a certain extent.
The proportions of the devil have shrunk so
much that the people have almost ceased to
fear him, and in the same degree as clerical
power has diminished, the conception of God has
assumed a grander aspect. Already the necessity of performing humanitarian labours has
been more fully recognised, and is by some
considered to be of almost equal importance to
the performance of the prescribed ceremonies.

Still the change goes on, gradually but slowly;
for there is a powerful giant who by his nega-
tion resists the decay of the pile of rubbish,
and the name of this giant is *Fashion*. It is
fashionable to support certain things, and therefore the masses support them.

"Is the progressive part of the world going to
wait until the legally appointed guardians of
the truth have found out the true value of the
treasure in their possession? Have we to wait
until they have cleaned the jewel from the dark
crust which they have permitted to accumulate around it for centuries? Messengers have
arrived from the East, the land of light, where
the sun of wisdom has risen, bringing with
them costly moonlight pearls and treasures of
liquid gold. Will their untold wealth be in-
trusted to the safe keeping of those who possess
the old and empty forms, or will the new wine
be filled in new casks, because the old ones are
rotten?

"But why should those who have begun to
see the dawn of the day close their eyes and
wait until the blind would inform them that
the sun is rising over the mountains? Is love
of the truth not strong enough to accomplish
that which the fear of a dread hereafter has
been able to accomplish? Cannot the enlightened classes establish academies, which

would offer all the advantages of orthodox convents without their disadvantages ? Could they
not establish a garden, where the divine lotus
flower of wisdom might grow and unfold its
leaves, sheltered against the storms of passion
raging beyond the walls, watered by the water
of truth, whose spring is within; where the
Tree of Life could unfold without becoming
encumbered by the weeds of credulity and
error; where the soul could breathe the pure
spiritual air, unadulterated by the odour of
the poison-tree of ignorance, unmixed with the
effluvia of decaying superstitions; a place where
this Tree of Life, springing from the roots of
the Tree of Knowledge, could grow and spread
its branches, far up in the invisible realm where
Wisdom resides, and produce fruits which cause
those who partake of them to become like gods
and immortal ? "

Here the Adept paused, as if in deep meditation; but after a moment of silence he said:
"Yes, by all means establish your theosophical
monastery, if you can find any inhabitants duly
prepared to enter it; for it will be easier to
introduce the truth into a house which is not
occupied, than into one which is occupied by its
enemies."

"But," I objected, "such an institution

would require an Adept as a teacher. Would you consent to teach?"

To this Theodorus answered, "Wherever there is a want, the supply will not fail to come, for *there is no vacuum in nature.*"

CHAPTER VIII

BLACK MAGIC

At this moment I heard again the sound of the invisible silver bell in the air, and the Adept, rising, said that he was called away for a few minutes, and invited me to remain until he should return. He left the laboratory, and I remained alone. I amused myself by looking over the book containing the *Secret Symbols of the Rosicrucians*, and my attention was attracted by the sign of a *Pentagram* turned upside down, so that the two points of the lower triangles pointed upwards. Suddenly a voice sounding behind my chair said : " In this symbol is contained eternity and time, god and man, angel and devil, heaven and ¦hell, the old and the new Jerusalem with all its inhabitants and creatures."

I turned, and I saw by my side a man with an extremely intelligent face, dressed in the habit of a monk. He excused himself for causing an interruption in my thoughts, and said that I seemed so deeply engaged in meditating over those figures that I had not observed his entrance.

The open countenance, the pleasant looks, and the intelligent expression of the face of my visitor at once gained my confidence; and I asked him who he was with whom I had the honour to speak.

"I am," said the stranger, "the *Famulus*, or, as you well may call it, the *Chela*, of Theodorus. They call me jocularly his intellectual principle, because I have to do his work when the old gentleman is asleep."

I found his remark very funny, and answered in a jocular way: "If you are called his intellectual principle, you are perhaps only a creation of his thought. I have seen so many strange things in this place, that I would not be surprised at anything, not even if you were to vanish before my eyes or turn into a snake or a devil."

To this the apparition replied: "As far as our external appearance is concerned, we are all forms produced by thought, and it is the privilege of men of a higher order to assume whatever form they find convenient for their purpose. Thus it may sometimes happen that the very devil appears in the shape of a saint for the purpose of deluding some gullible fool, and I know of cases where some jolly spirits

of nature have assumed the shapes of Christ
and the apostles for the purpose of amusing
themselves by misleading some ignoramus.
They usually succeed in such cases ; but I am
neither a devil nor an elemental spirit, and you
are neither an ignoramus nor a fool."

I found myself highly flattered by the favourable opinion expressed by my visitor, and I
did not wish to appear suspicious and thus
to weaken his faith regarding my power of
judging the character of a person at first sight.
Moreover, he had such a look of benevolence
that I did not wish to distrust him.   I therefore made him my bow, and said : "I have not
the least doubt about your honourable inten-
tions, and am quite sure that you are a reliable
guide."

" One cannot be careful enough in selecting
one's guides," continued the stranger.   "There
are at present so many false prophets and
guides.   All the world is at present crazy for
poking their noses into the mysteries of the
astral world.   Everybody wants to be taught
witchcraft and sorcery.   Secrets, which for thousands of years have been wisely kept hidden
before the eyes of the unripe and profane, are
now bawled out from the housetops and sold
at the market-place as objects of trade.   Hun-
dreds of self-appointed "masters" and guides

speculate upon the selfishness and ambitions of their disciples, and, the blind leading the blind, they both come to grief. If only all the seekers for truth were like you, they would not be deluded by false promises held out to them for attaining adeptship."

"I am really glad," I answered, "that you have discovered my purity and unselfishness of purpose, and I hope that, in consideration of my merits, you will be kind enough to show me some more of your occult secrets. Theodorus has already been preaching long sermons to me, and I listened to him with great patience; but now I want to see something substantial, and if possible learn how to perform some occult feats."

"Most willingly," said my companion. "I will do all I can for you, because you deserve by your unselfishness the patronage of all the Adepts."

So saying, he began to show me some of the curiosities of the laboratory, which contained many strange things. Of some of those I had read in books on alchemy; others were entirely new to me. At last we came to a closed shrine, and my curiosity led me to ask what it contained.

"Oh!" answered the monk, "this shrine contains some powders for fumigations, by the aid of which a man may see the Elemental Spirits of Nature."

"Indeed!" I exclaimed. "Oh, how I should like to see these lovely spirits! I have read a great deal about them in the books of Paracelsus; but I never had an opportunity of seeing them."

"They are not all of them lovely," said the monk. "The Elementals of earth have human forms. They are small, but they have the power to elongate their bodies. These gnomes and pigmies are usually ill-humoured and cross; and it is just as well to leave them alone, although sometimes they become very good friends of man, and may even show him hidden treasures and mines. The Elementals of air, the sylvans, are of a more agreeable nature; still we cannot rely upon their friendship. The salamanders, living in the element of fire, are ugly customers, and it is better to have nothing to do with them. But the nymphs and undines are lovely creatures, and they often associate with man."

"I wish I could see those beautiful watersprites," I said; "but I am inclined to believe that they belong to the realm of the fable. For many years, accounts given by seafaring men spoke of mermen and mermaids, which they insisted on having seen at a distance. They said that those people were like human beings, of whom the upper part resembled a man or a woman, while the lower part of their body was a fish. They told great stories about their beauty, their waving hair, and how finely they could sing; and they called them sirens, because it was said they could sing so well that men who heard their voices would become oblivious of everything else but their songs. At last, such a siren was caught; and it proved to be nothing else than a curious fish of the species called *Halicore catacca*, which at a distance may be mistaken for a man, on account of its colour, and which barks somewhat like a dog. Perhaps those undines and nymphs are also nothing but fishes."

"This is a most erroneous opinion, my dear sir," answered the monk. "The halicore is a fish; but the nymphs and undines are Elemental spirits of nature, living in the element of water, being, under ordinary circumstances, invisible to man, and not being able therefore to be caught in this manner. They are almost like human beings, but far more ethereal and beautiful; and under certain circumstances they may be seen by man. They may even attain a permanent material form and remain on land; and a case is even known in which a certain Count Stauffenberg married such a nymph on account of her beauty and lived with her for more than a year, until some stupid theologian frightened him by telling him that his wife was a devil. The count at that time had fallen in love with some good-looking peasant-girl, and so the interference of the preacher was welcome, and he took this as a pretext to drive his true wife away. But she revenged herself; and on the third day after his second marriage the count was found dead in his bed. These nymphs are very beautiful. They are strong in love, and are constant; but they are also said to be very jealous."

The more the monk spoke about the water-nymphs, the stronger grew my desire to see them. I asked him to put me in communication with those beautiful spirits; but he made all sorts of excuses, which, however, only served still more strongly to excite my curiosity.

"We are living here in this sinful world, and ought not to meddle with the inhabitants of another. We are all sinners and liable to succumb to temptations. These water-nymphs are continually seeking to be united with men, and they have good reason for it, because they have no immortal souls. Becoming united with man they form a link with his soul, and thus partake of his immortality."

"Why, then," I exclaimed, "do you hesitate

to conjure these beings? I would only be too happy to convey the gift of immortality to one of these beautiful spirits. Moreover, I would consider this as an act of charity and duty, and if such a nymph should insist upon marrying me, I can see no reason why I should object if she were amiable. Besides, it would be quite an extraordinary thing to have a water-nymph for a wife."

"They are not only very amiable," said the monk, "but they are also very obedient to their husbands. Such a water-nymph has no will of her own; she regards her husband as her saviour and god, never contradicts or scolds him, but is always ready to obey his commands, fulfil his wishes, and gratify his desires. She is very modest in her demands, needs no luxuries, and requires nothing except occasionally a short excursion to the seashore, which will cause you no expense whatever, because she has her own method of travelling."

I could restrain myself no longer, and earnestly begged the monk to make a fumigation with the mysterious powder. At last he consented. Putting a few pieces of dry maple tree bark and some dried leaves of laurel into a brazier, he added pieces of charcoal and lighted them. He then strewed some of the

mysterious powder, and a white smoke arose,
filling the room like a mist and with a very
sweet odour.   The objects in the laboratory
could soon be seen only dimly through that mist,
and finally disappeared altogether.   The walls
of the chamber were no more to be seen.   The
air seemed to take on a vibratory motion and
to become more dense; but, far from feeling
oppressed by this, I felt a great exhilaration
and satisfaction.   At last I knew I was in the
element of water, and was supported by it.
I was swimming, but my body was as light as
a feather, and it required no effort whatever
to keep me from sinking; it seemed as if the
water was my own element, as if I were born
in it.   A light shone directly above my head.
I rose up to the surface and looked around.   I
was in the midst of the ocean, dancing up and
down with the waves.   It was a bright moonlight night.   Right above me stood the full
moon and threw her silvery rays upon the
water, causing the ripples and the foamy crests
on the tops of the waves to sparkle like liquid
silver or diamonds.   Far in the distance appeared the coast with a mountain range, which
seemed familiar to me.   At last I recognised it
as the coast of the island of Ceylon, with the
range of mountains beyond Colombo and Galle;

surely I could not mistake, for I recognised the Adam's Peak.

Never shall I forget the agreeable sensation caused by that ethereal bath in the moonlit sea in the Indian Ocean. It seemed to me that at last my wish had been fulfilled, and that I was free of my mortal body and its weight; and yet I was myself. I could see no difference between the body I inhabited now and the one I inhabited before the fumigation was made, only my present body was so light that it seemed as if it would float in the air as easily as it did upon the water.

Listen! some faint sound is brought by the breeze; it seems to be a human voice. It comes nearer, and now I hear it plainly; it is the melodious song of a female voice. I look in the direction from which the sound seems to come, and I see three forms floating upon the waves, rising and sinking and coming nearer. They seem to play with each other, and as they approach I behold three beautiful females with long, waving hair; but the one in the middle surpasses the others in beauty. She seems to be the queen, for she wears a wreath of water-plants upon her head. Still nearer they come. Now they see me and stop. They consult together, but curiosity conquers

their fear. They come quite close and speak
to me. Their voices are full and melodious;
their language is foreign to me, and yet I
understand what they say. Having discovered
that I am a mortal, they appear as anxious
to cultivate my acquaintance as I am anxious
to be on friendly terms with them.

They invite me to go with them to their
home; they speak of their palace constructed
of beautiful shells among the coral-reefs in
the depths of the ocean; of the milk-white
pearls with which they have ornamented
the walls; of the azure blue of the waves
shining through the transparent walls of their
houses; and the curious things which no
mortal had ever seen. I object, and tell them
that I am mortal and that I could not live
in their own element; but the beautiful
queen, rising out of the water up to her waist,
smiles and shakes her charming head, and
fluid diamonds seem to stream from her waving
locks. "Come," she whispers; "no harm will
befall you, for my love shall protect you."
She extends her beautifully shaped arms towards me and touches my shoulder, and at
her touch my consciousness fades away. A
voluptuous sensation pervades my whole being.
I feel that I am dissolving in the element of

water; I only dimly hear the distant thunder of the breakers as they roll upon the sandy beach. I feel that my desire has been fulfilled — a moment, and I know nothing more.

IX

THE END

I HAVE little more to add to my tale. I awoke, and opening my eyes, I found myself stretched upon the moss, in the shadow of that mighty pine, where I had evidently fallen asleep. The sun stood still high above the western horizon, and far up in the sky two vultures described long drawn spirals in the air; and in their cries I seemed to recognise the voice of the queen of the nymphs. On the opposite side of the valley was still the rushing waterfall with the foaming basin, and the spray still rose in the air, and the water still sped over the moss-covered edge.

"Alas!" I exclaimed, "has all I have seen been nothing else than a dream? Has that which seemed so beautiful and real been merely an illusion of my brain, and have I now returned to real life? Why did I not die in the arms of the queen, and thus save myself this horrid awakening?"

I rose, and, as I rose, my eye fell upon the bud of a white lily sticking in a buttonhole of my coat. I could not believe my eyes, and suspected that I was again the victim of a hallucination. I grasped the lily. It did not vanish in my grasp; it was as real as the earth upon which I stood; it was of a kind which does not grow in these cold mountainous regions; it only grows where the air is mild and warm. I remembered the gold; I put my hand into my pocket, and there, among the few remaining silver pieces, I found a solid lump of gold as bright as the purest; but the little ruby pearls had dropped off from its surface and were lost. I then recollected the precious book which the Adept had promised to send to my room in the village inn; but somehow it seemed to me that I had committed an indiscretion during the absence of Theodorus by prying into the secrets of his laboratory and listening to the temptations of the Nymphs. I felt as if I did not deserve the favour, and was doubtful whether or not he would send me the book.

I flew rather than walked down the mountain, along the road leading toward the village. Little did I now care for the scenery; neither for the mountain tops, which were gilded by the rays of the setting sun, nor for the murmuring river. It grew dark ; and the full moon arose over the hills, looking exactly like the moon I had seen some hours before in the Indian Ocean. I calculated about the difference of time between Germany and Ceylon, and I found that indeed I might have seen the moon shine in the Bay of Bengal while the sun was shining in the Alps.

I arrived at O., little heeding the astonished looks of the villagers, who may have believed me insane as I hurried through the streets. I entered the inn, rushed upstairs to my room, and, as I entered, I saw upon the table the precious book, " The Secret Symbols of the Rosicrucians of the Sixteenth and Seventeenth Centuries." On the fly-leaf were written a few lines in pencil, saying :—

" Friend, I regret that you left our home so abruptly, and I cannot invite you to visit us again for the present. He who desires to remain in the peaceful valley must know how to resist all sensual attractions, even those of the Water Queen. Study this book practically ; bring the circle into a square. Mortify the metals ; calcinate and purify them of all residua. When you have succeeded, we shall

meet again. I shall be with you when you
need me.—Yours fraternally,

"THEODORUS."

It may be imagined that, in spite of my
fatigue, I did not go to sleep very early. I
walked up and down in my room, thinking
over the events of that memorable day. I
tried to find the line between the visible and
the invisible, between the objective and subjective, between dreams and reality, and I
found that there was no line, but that all
these terms are merely relative, referring not
merely to the conditions of things which
appear objective or subjective to ourselves,
but to our own conditions, and that while in
one state of existence certain things may
appear real to us and others illusive, in
another state the illusions become real, and
that which before seemed to be real is now
merely a dream. Perhaps our whole terrestrial
life will seem to be at the end nothing else
than a hallucination.

As I walked about the room I observed a
Bible belonging to my host lying upon a
cupboard. I felt an impulse to open it at
random and to see what it said. I did so,
and my eye fell upon the twelfth chapter of

the second epistle of the Apostle Paul, written
to the Corinthians, where it said :—

"*I knew a man in Christ, above fourteen
years ago (whether in the body or whether
out of the body I cannot tell ; God knoweth) ;
such a one was caught up into paradise and
heard unspeakable words, which it is not
lawful for a man to utter.*"

APPENDIX

SOME time after the first edition of the fore-
going pages appeared, an attempt was made in
republican Switzerland to carry into effect these
ideas. In the midst of the mountains, among
the most sublime and picturesque scenery, upon
a secluded hill near the shore of the most
beautiful Italian lake, extensive grounds were
purchased, and it was proposed to build a
house whose object it was to serve as a refuge
for those who wanted to cultivate spirituality
pure and simple, without any admixture of
priestcraft and superstition. It has not yet
been finally decided whether this undertaking
will be a success or a failure ; but the latter is
more than probable, as the method of thinking
in old dilapidated and dying Europe is too
narrowminded to permit of grasping such an
exalted idea.

We have asked the question whether there
would be any use or necessity for such

an institution, and received the following answer.

Upon the wide expanse of our social sea of life there is at present no dry spot to be found where the white dove of truth may rest her weary feet. The waves of contending self-interests clash together, being blown into fury by the storms of passion that rage in the human heart. Selfishness, deceit, and the follies of fashion are the kings that rule over the peoples of Europe, claiming as their tribute the immortality of their souls. The battle for superiority in the struggle for existence forces nations and individuals to use evil means; conventionalism forces men and women to be hypocritical; to be honest and unselfish means starvation and ruin; to be true and sincere means to incur social ostracism; sharpness, cunning, and policy are the vermin that infest the seat of divine wisdom; every social unit seeks to live and to thrive upon the ignorance of the rest. Thus man's whole time and attention is taken up with running after the worthless baubles and pleasures of this grossly material world, and the only redeeming angel, the true living faith—meaning the spiritual power to recognise spiritual truth—is fast driven away, taking with it the true light and leaving the world in darkness and despair.

Is there no one whose aspirations go higher than to enjoy the comforts of life, to eat and to drink, to be merry to-day and to die to-morrow, and who has ever been longing to find some way of escape from this great carnival, and to throw off the mask which he is forced to wear and which prevents him from seeing the truth? Do such persons never wish for a place where they might find refuge and enjoy communication with the God whose temples they are? Is such a desire to escape selfish, and is it necessary to hold out in the whirling dance that ends in the abyss of death?

It is truly said that spiritual strength grows only by resistance to temptations, but there must be a certain amount of strength before these temptations can be resisted and overcome by the power of the spirit. Is it selfish to seek to gain strength before the battle is entered? Is it selfish to wish for the possession of a certain amount of truth before one enters into an atmosphere filled with lies? Is it selfish if the gardener shelters a delicate plant in the hot-house until it grows strong enough to be set out in the garden and to encounter the vicissitudes of the climate? and is not spirituality such a delicate plant? Is it selfish for a child to remain in the mother's womb until it has gained strength to support

M

its own life, and is not the spiritual regeneration of man most difficult to accomplish? The world is full of spiritual miscarriages which have entered the battle with the devils that rule the world prematurely, and without being prepared for the fight; neither will the means for such a preparation be found in our churches and schools as they are constituted at present; where what is miscalled "religion" is carried on as a social amusement, and where not even the meaning of the term "spirituality" seems to be known. Those who wish to find the true light must rise up and embrace it with their whole heart and their whole being; they have no time to dream or to amuse themselves with the illusory treasures of the terrestial plane.

It is often said that people with spiritual aspirations should remain in the world and teach others, and do all the good they can; but what good can anyone do, if he has no knowledge of the consequences of his acts, and what knowledge can anyone teach to another if he knows nothing himself? Spiritual aspirations alone do not constitute spiritual knowledge; we must not only feel the truth but see it before we can know it ourselves. How can anyone teach the truth if the truth does not itself teach in and through him? There is already an abundance of preachers and teachers in the world who know the truth only from hearsay and from the reading of books; but it is only their light that shines, and not the light of the truth. What man needs is the Light itself, and not merely a description of it. There is no necessity to start a new sect with a new set of opinions and creeds; but there is a great necessity that a way should be found to teach mankind how they may open their eyes, so as to be able to perceive the truth themselves.

To those who know nothing about the possibility of attaining self-knowledge, imagining that God is incapable of teaching anything to the soul and that divine wisdom like man-made science is to be learned from man, the object of our institution will be incomprehensible. To those we can only say that it is not the object of this enterprise to furnish a retreat for misanthropes and hypochondriacs, where they may lead a lazy life, amusing themselves with bemoaning the wickedness of this sinful world; neither is it to be an infirmary for ghost-seers, visionaries, or dreamers, where they may revel to their hearts' content among the creations of their own fancy; nor is it to be a "school for occultism," where magic arts are taught to the fool; but it is intended to be a place where those who earnestly aspire to spirituality may find the external conditions necessary to cultivate it and to acquire the true "magic staff" that will securely support them on their voyage through eternity; namely, the power to recognise divine truth within their own selves—not by any capacity of their own, but by the power of the Light itself, which comes to all men if they are willing that the darkness should be driven away.

BIBLIOGRAPHY
of the
Works of Franz Hartmann
Published in English
COMPILED BY R. A. GILBERT

Hartmann's later writings in German have not been translated into English. He was a contributor to a number of esoteric periodicals, notably *The Theosophist*, *Lucifer* and *The Occult Review*. His most significant periodical contribution was his "Autobiography," printed in *The Occult Review*, vol. 7, no. 1, January 1908. Many of the quotations in the introduction to the present reprint are taken from this article, and from the obituary that appeared in a subsequent issue (vol. 16, no. 3, September 1912).

"Report of Observations Made during a Nine Months' Stay at the Head-Quarters of the Theosophical Society at Adyar (Madras), India." Madras, 1884.

Magic White and Black or The Science of Finite and Infinite Life containing Practical Hints for Students of Occultism. Boston & Madras, 1885; London, 1886. [Third edition, revised and enlarged, London, 1888.]

An Adventure Among the Rosicrucians. Boston, 1887. [New and revised edition, under the title *With the Adepts, an Adventure among the Rosicrucians*, London, 1910.]

The Life of Philippus Theophrastus, Bombast of Hohenheim, known by the name of Paracelsus, and the Substance of his Teachings. . . London, 1887. [Revised edition, London, 1896.]

Cosmology, or Universal Science. Containing the Mysteries of the Universe, regarding God, Nature Man, the Macrocosm and Microcosm, eternity and Time explained according to the Religion of Christ, by means of the Secret Symbols of the Rosicrucians of the Sixteenth and Seventeenth Centuries. Boston, 1888

The Life of Jehoshua, the Prophet of Nazareth. An Occult Study and a Key to the Bible, containing the History of an Initiate. Boston, 1889.

The Principles of Astrological Geomancy. The Art of Divining by Punctuation, according to Cornelius Agrippa and others. London & Boston, 1889.

The Talking Image of Urur. New York, 1890; London, 1890. [A humorous fantasy, incorporating Hartmann's experiences in California and India, with the real life characters only thinly disguised.]

In the Pronaos of the Temple of Wisdom, containing the History of the True and the False Rosicrucians. With an Introduction into the Mysteries of the Hermetic Philosophy. London & Boston, 1890.

"Capital Punishment." London, 1890 [pamphlet, *Theosophical Siftings*, vol. 3, no. 1].

The Life and Doctrines of Jacob Boehme, the God-

Taught Philosopher. Boston, 1891.

"The Philosophy of Self-Knowledge; or, the Mystery of the Three Worlds Revealing Itself in Man." London, 1892 [pamphlet, *Theosophical Siftings*, vol. 5, no. 6.].

Occult Science in Medicine. London, 1893.

Among the Gnomes: An Occult Tale of Adventure in the Untersberg. London, 1895; Boston, 1896.

Buried Alive: An Examination into the Occult Causes of Apparent Death, Trance and Catalepsy. Boston, 1895; London, 1896 [as *Premature Burial*].

"The Correlation of Spiritual Forces." New York, 1897 [pamphlet].